Case studies in organizational behaviour: teacher's manual

Edited by
Chris W Clegg, Nigel J Kemp and Karen Legge

Harper & Row, Publishers
London

Cambridge
Philadelphia
New York
San Francisco

Mexico City
São Paulo
Singapore
Sydney

Harper & Row Publishers Ltd
28 Tavistock Street
London WC2E 7PN

British Library Cataloguing in Publication Data

Case studies in organizational behaviour: teacher's manual.
  1. Organizational behaviour—Case studies
  I. Clegg, Chris W.   II. Kemp, Nigel J.
  III. Legge, Karen
  302.3′5′0722   HD58.7
  ISBN 0–06–318303–X

Typeset by Inforum Ltd, Portsmouth
Printed in Great Britain by
Antony Rowe Ltd., Chippenham

Contents

SECTION 3: INDUSTRIAL RELATIONS

Introduction

This book – a teacher's manual – is the companion volume to the book 'Case Studies in Organizational Behaviour'. In total, some 27 cases by 40 authors are presented. These cases are organized into three major sections: Organizational Behaviour; Personnel Management; and Industrial Relations. The reader is referred to the general introduction and to the introductions to each section within the case studies book, for a complete description of the organization of cases, interrelationships between them and the student tasks set.

For most cases this manual provides four brief sets of information. First, notes are provided on the appropriate *theoretical background* to each case, and key concepts are identified. Essentially, these represent the ideas the writer found useful in understanding the problems encountered. Second, a description is provided of *what actually happened* in each instance. This is particularly useful where organizations actively tried to solve their problems. Thirdly, a set of *answers* is given to the questions set. And, finally, the *references and further reading* follow each set of answers. These references provide examples and explanations of the theoretical concepts to be discussed, as well as referring the reader to additional published accounts of the cases described in the text.

We should make it clear that the answers and concepts provided in this manual are not offered as a set of 'truths'. They are intended as a guide and to provide some structure from which to organize and manage teaching sessions. We hope students and teachers will also develop and explore their own ideas from their own perspectives. It is possible, for example, that users may wish to develop their own questions and answers from a number of cases, building up their own cross-references within and across the three major sections. As an aid to this task we reproduce here the matrix of cases and themes presented in the introduction to the case studies text (Table 2). This matrix presents the case title, the major issues in the particular case and the interrelationships between cases. From this the user can check the main themes which are relevant in any particular case, as well as plan an overall course of teaching. We hope the resulting sessions are stimulating and enjoyable for all concerned.

Table 2 Matrix of cases and topics

#	CASE	TOPIC	SETTING	1	2	3	4	5	6	7	8	9	10	11	12	13	14	15	16	17	18	19	20	21	22	23	24	25	26	27
				Job Design	Man-machine interface	Stress	Supervisory Behavior	Managerial Style & Appraisal	Information & Control Systems	Decision-Making	Power and Politics	Organizational Consulting & Development	Small Businesses: Family Firms & management	Organizational Structure	Absence & Turnover	Selection & Recruitment	Training and Skills	Health & Safety at Work	Redundancy	Management Development	Payment Systems	Equal Opportunities	Negotiating Behaviour	Collective Bargaining	Industrial Disputes	A Lock-Out	Strike Organization	New Technology	Participation & Communications	Trade Union Democracy
1	Fab Sweets Ltd.	Job Design	Confectionery Firm	●		○	○		○						○		○				○	○								
2	Oilco	Man-machine Interface	Marketing and Distribution Division of Oil Company	○	●				○					○			○											○	○	
3	Stress amongst Crane Drivers	Stress	Construction Companies	○	○	●										○	○	○											○	
4	Photoproducts UK	Supervisory Behaviour	'Greenfield' Film Processing Factory	○			●	○						○			○											○		
5	Administrators in the NHS	Managerial Style and Appraisal	National Health Service	○				●	○								○												○	
6	Tewes Ltd.	Information and Control Systems	Confectionery Firm	○			○		●	○	○			○						○									○	
7	British Rail	Decision-Making	Nationalised Industry							●	○												○	○	○					
8	TVN	Power and Politics	Independent Television Company					○		○	●			○						○								○		
9	John Player and Sons	Organizational Consulting and Development	Cigarette Manufacturing and Distribution					○				●		○						○									○	
10	J. & S. Nicholson Ltd.	Small Businesses: Family firms and management	Construction Company								○	○	●	○																
11	Gamma Appliances	Organizational Structure	Manufacturing and Marketing of Electronic Office Equipment							○	○	○	○	●					○											

		CASE	TOPIC	SETTING		1	2	3	4	5	6	7	8	9	10	11	12	13	14	15	16	17	18	19	20	21	22	23	24	25	26	27
CASES																																
PERSONNEL	12	The Absentee Bus Crews	Absence and Turnover	Coal Valley Bus Company	12	○			○		○						●	○					○								○	
	13	HAL	Selection and Recruitment	Manufacturing and Distribution of Electronics	13						○							●	○			○	○	○								
	14	Royal Navy	Training and Skills	Naval Training Establishments	14	○	○											○	●											○		
	15	Texchem	Health and Safety at Work	Textile, Chemical and Plastics Manufacturing Factory	15	○	○				○		○			○			○	●						○					○	
MANAGEMENT	16	Office Engineering Company	Redundancy	Manufacturing Company	16			○				○	○			○					●					○	○					
	17	British Rail	Management Development	Nationalised Industry	17									○		○			○			●										
	18	Mayfly Garments Ltd.	Payment Systems	Manufacturing Company	18	○			○				○				○	○	○				●	○								
	19	Champion Oils Ltd.	Equal Opportunities	Refining and Production in a Process Plant	19								○						○				○	●	○	○						○
INDUSTRIAL RELATIONS	20	Micklethwaite Brewery Plc.	Negotiating Behaviour	Brewing Industry	20							○											○		●	○						
	21	Car Co.	Collective Bargaining	Vehicle Manufacture and Assembly	21	○				○			○								○		○		○	●				○	○	
	22	Small Metals Factory	Industrial Disputes	Engineering Factory	22				○	○			○										○		○	○	●					○
	23	Times Newspapers Ltd.	A Lock-Out	Fleet Street	23					○			○												○	○	○	●	○	○		○
	24	Steel Strike	Strike Organization	Rotherham, S. Yorkshire Strike Committee	24								○												○	○	○		●			○
	25	'RM' Division	New Technology	Manufacturing Company	25	○							○					○	○				○		○	○				●		
	26	Kitchenco	Participation and Communications	Manufacturing Company	26					○		○							○				○			○					●	
	27	Union Government and Union Democracy	Trade Union Democracy	Transport and General Workers Union	27						○	○	○			○										○					○	●

SECTION 1: Organizational Behaviour

CASE 1 Job Design: Fab Sweets Ltd.
Nigel Kemp, Chris Clegg and Toby Wall

Theoretical Background

This includes the following: (a) socio-technical systems theory (SST) [key concepts of which are an open system and joint optimization] (see, for example, Miner 1982); (b) a job characteristics model (JCM) [key concepts of which are autonomy, variety, feedback, task significance and task identity] (Hackman and Oldham 1976). SST's major concern is system-based changes, e.g. autonomous group working; while JCM's major concern is individually based changes, e.g. job enlargement or enrichment. This approach is a reaction against Taylorism [key concepts of which are fragmentation, specialization and hierarchical control] and its hypothesized deleterious effects (low QWL, poor quality, absenteeism and labour turnover). Both SST and JCM predict an improved quality of working life for employees and organizational benefits (e.g. improved organizational climate, lower absenteeism and turnover, higher quality and possible productivity increases). Note: research evidence in support of these effects is mixed and critics point to its possible costs (e.g. lost jobs? labour intensification? enhanced management control?) (see Kelly 1982).

What Actually Happened

Using the SST and JCM concepts, four major changes were implemented over a three year period, viz. (i) the removal of the physical barrier (this required the introduction of a cooling system) between production and packing to improve integration and to provide a whole task; (ii) the creation of two semi-autonomous work groups responsible for the complete production process from raw materials to finished sweets and including day to day operational decision making; hence (iii) the removal of supervisory roles, leaving only the departmental manager and a clerical assistant; and (iv) improved target and feedback systems.

Direct Outcomes
These have been evaluated through a range of psychological, organizational and performance measures. They include the following: (i) shopfloor control over the daily operational decisions; (ii) a 'flatter' management structure; (iii) the teams described their jobs as incorporating more autonomy, task identity and feedback and reported higher levels of job satisfaction and lower levels of mental strain; (iv) the changes in the grading system resulted in some pay increases; (v) there was a reported increase in motivation and a 22% rise in overall productivity; (vi) the information systems became useful to the shop floor.

Organizational Ramifications

(i) The production planning department was required to balance yearly production plans so as not to disrupt the group working system and stable environment in HB. (ii) The marketing department had to cope with an increased output from HB. (iii) The engineering department had to become more responsive to HB in both preventive and emergency maintenance. (iv) The supervisors and middle management elsewhere in the organization became concerned about job security and loss of control of the production process. This resulted (v) in the restriction of the job redesign exercise to HB (see Wall and Clegg 1981; Kemp et al. 1980; Clegg and Fitter, 1978).

Answers

(See also comments above.)

1 Solution (d) most appropriate, followed by (a); (b) and (c) in this instance would be counterproductive.
2 Structural changes to job content and decision making; also attention to interpersonal processes through group or social skill training.
3 If solution (d) in question 1 is adopted, (a) should both increase given adequate technical support, target systems, commitment and knowledge of the production process by operators. Increased levels of satisfaction should reduce (b), but note the possible effect of intervening variables (e.g. domestic responsibilities, journey to work, alternative employment opportunities). If solutions (b) or (c) (in question 1 above) were to be adopted, note the potentially negative consequences.
4 Management style needs to be more considerate with supportive control exercised at a distance, i.e. delegation of authority to the work groups with management maintaining the boundaries of the system.
5 (a) With regard to selection, the measures need to include the development of criteria appropriate to group working (e.g. potential for multi-skilling, cooperativeness and sociability), the involvement of employees in the selection process; with regard to the training, social skills induction training should be introduced to enhance cohesiveness, as should technical training on and off job in multi-skilling.
(b) Both target and feedback systems need to be accurate, fair, immediate and comprehensible.
(c) Multi-skilling requires commensurate pay and grading increases, but note the possible differential disputes elsewhere in the plant and problems with 'agreed' demarcation and responsibility lines. Also, the 'flatter' structure may result in the loss of some supervisory promotion possibilities, with some consequent dissatisfaction and/or turnover.
(d) Joint optimization. The physical layout should mirror the production process and allow for integrated group working. Note the importance of machine reliability and hence the importance of preventive maintenance.
(e) Training (consisting of group process, interpersonal and social skills training, and management development) for interpersonal problems; participative exercises (e.g. briefing groups; quality circles) and information systems for communication problems.
(f) Cross functional regular meetings at both management and operator/supervisory level could be initiated; liaison roles are another means of improving interdepartmental relationships.
6 Use a participative approach (but note the costs, e.g. time, in doing so).

7   (i) A stable, committed workforce, and a low turnover. There is a need, therefore,
for long-term planning. A change is needed in job descriptions at all levels to reflect
the new system of work organization. (ii) More democracy is needed within the
company and in job-related decisions – but note the possibility of a supervisory or
middle management backlash. (iii) The information needs to be reliable and available; the requirement is for forecasting and planning rather than 'fire-fighting'.

References and Further Reading

Clegg C W Fitter M (1978) Information systems: the Achilles heel of job redesign, Personnel
    Review, 7: 5–11
Hackman J R Oldham G R (1976) Motivation through the design of work: test of a theory.
    Organizational Behavior and Human Performance, 15: 250–279
Kelly J E (1982) Scientific Management, Job Redesign and Work Performance, Academic Press
Kemp N J Clegg C W Wall T D (1980) Job redesign: content, process and outcomes, Employee
    Relations, 2: (5) 5–14
Miner J B (1982) Theories of Organizational Structure and Process, Dryden Press
Wall T D Clegg C W (1981) A longitudinal field study of group work redesign, Journal of
    Occupational Behaviour, 2: 31–49

CASE 2   The Man–Machine Interface: Oilco
Leela Damodaran and Susan Pomfrett

Theoretical Background

This includes the following: (a) socio-technical systems theory – the key concepts of
which are open systems and task interdependencies – and (b) concepts of acceptability.
With regard to (b), the usage of technological systems has frequently fallen short of the
expectations of system providers. Research concerned with identifying reasons for this
shortfall (Eason et al. 1974) revealed that acceptability of the man–machine interface
from the users' viewpoint is a crucial determinant of usage.

Empirical research into usage of computer systems by a variety of user types
(managers, specialists and clerks) shows that users typically evaluate systems on the
basis of identifiable factors. These factors include the relevance and appropriateness of
the computer service for the *user's own job*, the design of the environment surrounding
computer peripherals and of hardware features (i.e. traditional man–machine interface
issues), the software interface, the quality of user support, and finally the longer term
job design and organizational effects of the system. These characteristics can be
grouped to provide four indices of user acceptability:

1   Task match
2   Ease of use   } Early, immediate and enduring
3   User support   } impact upon the user
4   Indirect consequences   Long term effects upon the user

For a short description of user acceptability see Damodaran (1981). To understand
the empirical research which led to the formulation of the indices see Eason et al.
(1974).

What Actually Happened

As a result of studying the man–machine interface within the framework of the socio-technical systems theory and the acceptability concepts outlined above, it became clear that in principle, the *concept* of electronic mail was acceptable and, although there were some problems with this particular system, it also was acceptable. The major problems arose because of the particular circumstances under which electronic mail was used in the experiment. Thus, the following decisions were made: (i) to withdraw the electronic mail system from the north-eastern region; (ii) to run the electronic mail system on the company's own computer; (iii) to choose future networks of users extremely carefully; (iv) to acknowledge the importance of the design of the man–machine interface; (v) to seek specific improvements to the immediate man–machine interface, by making hardware and software changes, and finding solutions to the technical problems of data transmission.

This meant that the north-eastern region was required to 'give up' a tool that had at least been partially useful. Thus it was returning to the pre-trial situation with all its original problems, e.g. difficulty in contacting fieldstaff. On a more general level manning the system 'in house' was important both as a demonstration of commitment and as an attempt to improve ease of use. It was felt that the experiment had been successful in that it had promoted learning: the fact that the technological and man–machine interface problems were acknowledged, improved the ability of the company to implement successful systems.

Answers

1 Electronic communication provides a direct and immediately accessible link which does not require the receiver to be available at the same time. It relies solely upon the written word and provides a hard copy record of the communication. The system provides an easy means of mass communication, and does not require knowledge of the location of the recipient. Electronic communication is usually provided by a system incorporating limited filing facilities for user.

2 There is often some overlap between categories. As regards *ease of use*, difficulties can be experienced in using the keyboard, setting up portable terminals, getting a 'good' telephone line that is not engaged, in finding a good work station at home, with using the edit and file commands, also one can receive poor or erroneous messages. As regards *task match*, there are problems with the network population (e.g. the accounts centre offices that did not need to initiate communication, the need for a critical mass of users), problems with the accuracy and reliability when transmitting numbers, and the problem of not being able to go back and send a message when the system has prompted use (could be classed as ease of use). As regards *user support*, there are problems of support for the office staff, and from poor or erroneous messages. As regards *indirect consequences*, concern was expressed over using computers at home (e.g. interference by/with other electrical devices); there were also fears of extra work and the 'Big Brother' syndrome, etc.

3 Making these interfaces easier to use and more closely matched to the task of the user. Numerous specific possibilities, e.g. making the acoustic coupling easier to use, improving dialogue with the system – making erroneous messages understandable, etc. (See Damodaran, Simpson and Wilson 1980.)

4 Critical mass becomes much less important and the choice of user population is less critical. People have to contact the computer for every day work. Usage will be more frequent and messages more likely to be read and actioned.

5   The population was large and crossed intra-organizational boundaries, and the tasks required the communication of numerical information. Another network was set up with different characteristics. The users were personnel managers who did not need to transmit such numeric data so corruption was not such a problem. The network was relatively small and consisted of users who performed similar functions but between whom conventional communication was difficult. The system was used to very good effect.

6   (a) In reality, none of these options was chosen; **d** is nearest. No system was used until interface improved. Involved changing user population to improve task match whilst improving system to enable use with a wider population. No point in **e**; **a** was not warranted; the interface was not good enough for **b**; **c** would have been possible but cost of running a system with major interface problems would be high.

(b) The answer depends on that given in (a). It is important to recognize the operational aspects of the decision (efficiency, etc.), motivational and attitudinal aspects (e.g. do people like such systems?), and structural aspects (e.g. does automation provide opportunities for changing organizational structure?)

7   The issues here are strategic. Since electronic mail is only one part of the office automation programme, it must be considered in a wider context. A human factors policy is needed as part of this strategy to prevent the installation of systems not acceptable to users. The policy needs to specify criteria for equipment and workplace design, job design, training, health and safety as well as role of support groups. Such a policy needs formalizing and resourcing (time, expertise and money). It would then need translating into action plans which assign the responsibilities and resources required. The main task is to ensure office automation systems are implemented in a planned and systematic manner taking regard of technical, organizational and human aspects.

References and Further Reading

Coombs M Alty J (eds) (1981) Computer Skills and the User Interface, Academic Press

Damodaran L (1981) Measures of user acceptability, in Health Hazards of VDUs? edited by B G Pearce, John Wiley

Damodaran L Simpson A Wilson P A (1980) Designing Systems for People, National Computer Centre

Dzida A Herda S Itzfeldt T W (1978) User-perceived quality of interactive systems, IEEE Transactions on Software Engineering, SE-4: 270–275

Eason K D Damodaran L Stewart T F M (1974) A survey of man–computer interaction in commercial applications, LUTERG Report No. 144, Department of Human Sciences, Loughborough University of Technology

Eason K D Stewart T F M Damodaran L (1977) Case studies in the impact of computer based information systems upon management, Report No. DHS 243, Department of Human Sciences, Loughborough University of Technology

Kolf F (1980) Guidelines for the organisational implementation of information systems – concepts and experiences with the PORGI Implementation Handbook, in The Human Side of Information Processing, edited by N B Andersen, North Holland

CASE 3   Stress: Stress Among Crane Drivers
Cary Cooper and Mike Kelly

Theoretical Background

(i) There has been a growth of interest in, and pressure for job satisfaction and improvements in quality of working life. (ii) There is medical and related evidence of the costs to industry of stress and stress-related illness (e.g. Cooper and Payne 1980). (iii) Five broad areas of work stress have been identified (Cooper 1981): workload, work role ambiguity and/or conflict, interpersonal conflict, career prospects, and the home–work interface. The stress-related consequences have been identified as ill-health, job dissatisfaction and apathy, absenteeism and labour turnover. (iv) The case study also introduces the consequence of above-average accident levels, linked to workload and interpersonal conflict, plus a personality dimension. (v) Accident theory (Kay 1978) relates accident levels to changes from automatic behaviour to cruder stimulus–response behaviour, and pressured operations. (vi) There are difficulties of definition and measurement of stress levels and effects. (vii) For change strategies relevant to the case, see Ottaway (1979) and the work of Lewin (1951); normative and/or re-educative strategy was recommended to the companies, relating to attitude change as the key to stress management, plus job redesign elements such as rotation and enlargement.

What Actually Happened

The study was carried out over a six-month period in 1983 and the research indicated that a larger study, either looking in-depth at a number of accident incidents, or using on-site physical stress test techniques, would be advisable. However, seven main recommendations were made to the companies as the first stages in the management of stress levels in operators. These were as follows: (i) the introduction and development of more comprehensive accident level monitoring related to the different crane types, identifying patterns and developing safety awareness among operators and others; (ii) the introduction of consciousness-raising training and on-site publicity aimed at developing awareness for all personnel, focusing upon stress and fatigue factors and their cumulative effects; (iii) the identification of job demands and relating recruitment and selection procedures to those demands; (iv) the introduction of changes in work patterns, for example, to recognize particular danger situations by changed routines and/or technology, as when a driver is operating out of sight of the handling operation; (v) the introduction of job rotation and enrichment to develop and support higher job satisfaction levels; (vi) the buying-in of training sessions for team awareness and team development to form more effective co-worker relationships; (vii) the development of job and personal counselling skills in supervisory staff.

Company reactions varied from distinct lack of enthusiasm to some involvement by big companies in developing safety publicity and short training sessions. One of these larger organizations is reviewing work routines, though job rotation is not considered a 'realistic option'.

Answers

1   The Factory Inspectorate could not find an exact cause of this accident. They identified three possibilities: operation outside load/radius limits of the crane; incorrect setting of outriggers for ground conditions; ground at pit edge giving way.

Stresses on John included some or all of the following: work pressure having lost a day due to crane failure; stop–start patterns of work with frequent positional changes; isolation from, yet dependence on co-workers; risk both to co-workers and schoolchildren.

No definite answer is possible but the stresses upon John probably contributed to the accident. More generally it is our view that stress significantly contributes to accidents of this kind, although evidence is not conclusive. (See Cooper and Kelly 1984.)

2   Consider assumptions behind use of term 'stress' and some alternative conceptions. Stress is complex and involves attitude and experience as well as behaviour and cognition. It has physical, mental and emotional components. In the case, stress has a 'common sense' and laymen's definition using self-report techniques. If the opportunity arose, detailed research could incorporate cognitive performance indices, physiological measures and more detailed examination of individual differences and critical incidents. Such studies, however, are exceptionally difficult and rare in applied settings.

3   The measures taken could include the following: (i) recognize the nature of problem and its scope (pending future research); (ii) review the work organization with a view to reducing stress (e.g. job rotation, job enlargement, team working); (iii) review the selection procedures (e.g. are some personalities more suitable for work of this kind?); (iv) examine the training needs of crane operators, co-workers and supervisors, especially regarding safety; (v) develop counselling opportunities especially for the operators under stress; (vi) consider ways of reducing the pressures of deadlines.

4   The actions could include the following: (i) demonstrate the nature, scope and both the operational and financial consequences of the problem, i.e. make the problem concrete and significant; (ii) relate the problem to the ways in which building sites operate; (iii) in specific instances widen the debate by illustrating the costs and benefits of this method of working and then consider the alternative methods along with different profiles of costs and benefits; (iv) through wide discussions change safety from a perceived cost to a benefit and an indication more generally of good management and efficiency; (v) education and attitude change is required for operators and their supervisors and the site managers; (vi) the process will be helped by clear unambiguous support and leadership from a senior manager in an authoritative position. See Bennis et al. (1976). Clearly changes of this kind require resources (e.g. time for discussions).

5   Production levels may fall in the short term but should return to the same or higher levels in time, since even minor accidents are very costly for production. In the short term safety consciousness may prevent people taking 'short-cuts', but may also act as a pressure for better organization and planning of the work. Quality should not be adversely affected and may improve. Work organization may require better co-ordination to prevent panics to meet deadlines. It is also possible to achieve greater flexibility if people are trained for job rotation or team-working. Management style will change if people become aware of the stress and accident problems. Managers and supervisors will need to be person- as well as task-centred. The recognition of stress and support for people in stressful roles will be required. At the same time more planning and better coordination of resources will be required. Overall the manager's job will be harder, with a move away from 'fire-fighting'. This will require management training and development. Also required will be clear and effective two-way communication processes.

References and Further Reading

Bennis W G Benne K D Chin R (1976) The Planning of Change, 3rd edition, Holt, Rinehart & Winston

Cooper C L (1981) The Stress Check, Spectrum

Cooper C L Kelly M (1984) Stress among crane drivers, Journal of Occupational Medicine 26(8): 575–578

Cooper C L Payne R (eds) (1978) Stress at Work, John Wiley

Cooper C Payne R (1980) Current Concerns in Occupational Stress, John Wiley

Kay H (1978) Accidents: some facts and theories, in Psychology at Work, edited by P B Warr, Penguin

Kemp N J Clegg C W Wall T D (1980) Job redesign: content, process and outcomes, Employee Relations 2: 5–14

Lewin K (1951) Frontiers in group dynamics, in Field Theory in Social Science, edited by D Cartwright, Greenwood Press

Ottaway R (ed.) (1979) Change Agents at Work, Associated Business Press

Warr P B (ed.) (1978) Psychology at Work, Penguin

CASE 4 Supervisory Behaviour: Photoproducts UK
Sheila Rothwell

Theoretical Background

Leadership theories and 'contingency' theories have been applied to the analysis of the supervisory role. Consideration of its historical development out of the foreman/gang-leader/subcontractor role versus deputizing for the owner manager role throws some light on reasons for particular expectations, or confusion (Child 1982). Evidence of the erosion of the function – by technology (Thurley 1973; Buchanan and Boddy 1983), by work groups, and by managers – seen over time, and in the case. Child's study of supervisors (becoming unionized) in traditional engineering and food plants in the Midlands suggests four main future role options: abolition; clarification and bureau-cratization; managerial; technological/professional. Thurley and Wirdenius (1973) suggest a 'contingency' analysis of roles via critical dimensions of task environment and individual role: (1) (a) continuous process and/or unit technology and (b) routine and/or programme decision making; (2) (a) supervisory role highly and/or traditionally struc-tured and (b) high or low individual work involvement. Does the need to cope creatively with unexpected crises and contingencies contradict the possibility of role definition? Four choices of change strategy are based on: power; training method; empirical or rational analysis; action-centred change – evidence of all approaches can be found in the Greenfields case at different stages.

Literature is available on job design and motivation (Vroom and Deci 1970); on work groups (Hill 1974); on role conflict (Kahn et al. 1964); on introduction of new tech-nology (Rothwell and Davidson 1982) and the extent to which it increases management control, deskills jobs, etc. (Wood 1982); on organizational change strategy (Margerison 1978); and on site relocation. These are all also relevant.

What Actually Happened

(a) The numbers of group supervisors were reduced by abolishing the role of shift group supervisor and instead having one group supervisor, who works days only and to whom all report.

(b) It is planned that shift engineers and supervisors rotate shifts over a period so they get to know all teams. As an experiment, an engineering craftsman is attached to one of the production teams on each shift.

(c) A two-week residential training course was organized off site for the whole supervisory team. Four weeks before the course, four groups of three supervisors (production and engineering) were given a project of 'How do I motivate people?' on which to make a 30 minute group presentation at the course. The senior supervisor took a leading part in several sessions. Other speakers included a representative from the Industrial Society, behavioural specialists, and an academic researcher to report on other studies of supervisors' roles. Case studies of two other company experiences with team working were presented. There was an attempt to be much more workplace and problem oriented than at the previous, more theoretical, course.

(d) There was clarification of the supervisory role as a 'people'-oriented one and that the task of supervisors was to achieve 'productivity through people'. Emphasis was placed on supervising teams rather than individuals: a 'people as a group' theme.

Answers

1   See (a) above. As team working develops the need for supervision should diminish. Computerized information systems incorporate several of the control, coordination, and work allocation functions.
2   A 'pilot' experiment is often a good way to test a possible solution (see (b) above), but careful monitoring and evaluation is needed. See also 6 below.
3   See (d) above. Selection criteria will need to include greater emphasis on 'ability to motivate', and experience of team coordination. Technical abilities in both the 'practical' aspect and an understanding of the computer information system will still be critical, though highly motivated work groups tend to experience fewer technical breakdowns. 'Team leaders' should be obtaining some of the necessary skills. Rotation of the team leader role might develop operator potential, but would mean the loss of a (small) promotion post (cf. Japanese methods).
4   Greenfields' supervisors have gained their experience and expertise in a very different location. They have survived a wide range of family, personal and job changes in the last few years. Their technical skills, by which they had once achieved status, now seem to be less important. An 'indirect', 'hands-off' style is particularly difficult to grasp and can lead to 'withdrawal' from the role (cf. Child and Partridge 1982). Continued support in this will be needed to enable them to change their own behaviour and that of others. Some computer skills are also necessary – both technical and cognitive. Literature on leadership style supports participative approaches but the concept has tended to be hierarchical and directive.
5   See (c) above. Two weeks, rather too long a period, but it demonstrated the importance of the supervisors to the company and developed greater interpersonal confidence and understanding. More use of practical role-play exercises is needed; and more senior management involvement to help build up partnership with supervisors and develop own training and coaching skills (Jones 1982).
6   (a) Regular meetings of the supervisory team (despite shift problems) with the group supervisor to develop scope of roles and discuss problems.

(b) Attention to trade union and pay grading issues, e.g. integrated pay structure? factory bonus? union branch? shop steward elections and roles?

(c) Should output responsibility be shifted to work group? Accountability without power exists now but the removal of responsibility could further diminish the supervisors' status.

7 Organizational change is the primary cause – moving to a new site, increased competitive pressure, new factory management, conscious attempts at a new approach. Technological change added an extra dimension – and threat – and in turn necessitated other organizational change. Change is likely to continue as information becomes more centralized and prospects of organizational integration increase (see Child 1984).

8 There is scope for job enrichment; more attention should be given to pay systems; there is a need to give supervisors training in advance of or alongside operators; the effects on status should be noted.

References and Further Reading

Buchanan D A Boddy D (1983) Organisation in the Computer Age, Gower

Child J (1984) Organisation: A Guide to Problems and Practice, 2nd edition, Harper & Row

Child J Partridge B (1982) Lost Managers: Supervisors in Industry and Society, Cambridge University Press

Hill S (1974) Norms, workgroups and power, British Journal of Industrial Relations 12: 213–226

Institute of Personnel Management (1980) Personnel Policies an New Technology, Institute of Personnel Management

Jones A (1982) Partnering the supervisor, Management Today, May

Kahn R L Wolfe D M Quinn R P Snoek J D Rosenthal R A (1964) Organisational Stress, John Wiley

Margerison C (1978) Influencing Organisational Change, Institute of Personnel Management

Rothwell S Davidson D (1982) New technology and manpower utilisation, Employment Gazette, June and July

Thurley K Wirdenius H (1973) Supervision: A Reappraisal, Heinemann

Thurley K (1973) Computers and supervisors, in Sociology of the Workplace, edited by M Warner, Allen & Unwin

Vroom V H and Deci E L (1970) Management and Motivation, Penguin

Wood S (ed.) (1982) The Degradation of Work?, Hutchinson

Woodward J (1965) Industrial Organisation: Theory and Practice, Oxford University Press

CASE 5 Managerial Style and Appraisal: Administrators in the NHS
Rosemary Stewart and Pauline Wingate

Answers

The following different approaches can be used either alone or together to analyse this case study:

1 The main method suggested is the model of demands, constraints and choices developed by the author to explain the fact that individuals in similar jobs may spend their time doing very different kinds of work. *Demands* are what anybody in the job would have to do and cannot avoid doing because the penalties of not doing so would be too great. In many managerial jobs, and particularly senior ones like the district administrator, the core of demands is small. *Constraints* are the factors that limit what the jobholder can do. *Choices* are the opportunities in the job for one jobholder to do different work from another and to do it in different ways.

Managerial jobs can be described as flexible spaces that are only partially occupied by any one jobholder.

2 The extent to which the jobholder meets the expectations of the role set. In using this approach account also needs to be taken of the expectations that the jobholder created, as Kieser has said: 'That manager is effective who is able to build up high expectations with his role senders and to fulfil these expectations he evoked.' (Role senders are those who convey expectations as to how the jobholder should behave.)

3 By analysing the output requirements for the job and considering the extent to which the jobholder meets these. In longer discussions on this case time could be spent trying to define what are the output requirements of the job.

4 By considering whether the jobholder is good at optimizing the contributions of others.

Using one type of approach (demands, constraints and choices) one would identify the choices that the DA takes and the area of the job space that is unoccupied, of which the prime example is adequate attention to administration, particularly paperwork for committees. But remember that no one can occupy all the space, so it is a judgement of his priorities. As head of administration he is inadequate but criticisms of this are muted because he is generally liked and his other abilities are admired.

Using a second type of approach (expectations), for which the book by Machin (1981) is additional reading, one would note the areas in which he did, and those where he did not, meet expectations, and whose expectations were best met. One should also consider what kind of expectations he has established in others of what he will do.

Using a third type of approach (outputs) one should identify that there are some concrete outputs that can be identified, such as agenda papers in time for meetings, although they are outputs that the DA is responsible for but could delegate. There are other qualitative outputs of varying degrees of imprecision, such as well informed DHA members, efficient DMT meetings although that responsibility is shared, and morale factors explored below.

Using a fourth type of approach one should start from the assumption that an effective manager is one who optimizes the contributions of all those with whom he or she works (Belbin 1981). The DA fails to do this in terms of effectiveness of meetings and their preparation but is clearly good at arousing loyalty and hard work amongst his staff, and also contributes to knitting the DMT together. But remember the criticisms of his lacking a clear sense of direction and being too willing to placate.

Questions 5–7 should be used to explore what can be done to capitalize on the DA's strengths and to minimize his weaknesses, rather than on expecting him to change radically.

References and Further Reading

Belbin R M (1981) Management Teams, Heinemann

Boyatzis R E (1982) The Competent Manager: A Model for Effective Performance, John Wiley

Cameron K (1980) Critical questions in assessing organizational effectiveness, Organizational Dynamics, Autumn

Drucker P E (1967) The Effective Executive, Heinemann

Kieser A (1984) How does one become an effective manager? in Leaders and Managers: International Perspectives on Managerial Behaviour and Leadership, (eds) J G Hunt D Hosking C A Schriesheim and R Stewart, Pergamon Press, pp. 90–94

Machin J (1981) Expectations Approach: Improving Managerial Communications and Perform-
ance, McGraw-Hill
Stewart R (1982) Choices for the Manager: A Guide to Managerial Work and Behaviour,
McGraw-Hill, Chapters 1, 2, 8, 11, 12 (of which 1 and 11 are the minimum)
Stewart R Smith P Blake J Wingate P (1980) The District Administrator in the National Health
Service, King Edward's Hospital Fund for London, distributed by Pitman

CASE 6 Information and Control Systems: Tewes Ltd.
Mike Fitter and Chris Clegg

Theoretical Background

This includes the following: (a) socio-technical systems theory [key concepts of which are an open system and joint optimization] (see, for example, Miner 1982); (b) job characteristics model [the key concept here being feedback] (see Hackman and Oldham 1976); (c) the role of information systems in job redesign (see Oldham and Hackman 1980); (d) the functional or dysfunctional consequences of information systems and the need for appropriate structures (see Galbraith 1973); (e) the need to match systems to people's cognitive models (see Sime and Coombs 1983); and (f) the wider aspects of information and control systems (see Tricker 1976) – [key concepts of which are strategic, operating and control decisions; performance assessment and optimization].

What Actually Happened

A new information and control system was required for use *within* the department. Eight design criteria were specified (see 4 below). The post of clerical assistant was created to administer this system (see 3 below). The new system was very effective at providing timely and appropriate feedback to the teams to allow them to monitor and control their performance (see 6 below). It also had repercussions outside of the department (see 8 below). (See Clegg and Fitter 1978.)

Answers

1 The information system was slow (2–3 weeks after the week in question); in summary form (for a whole department, for a whole week); complicated and not understood; irregular and critical (usually when performance was low); and systematically inaccurate, unfairly depressing performance levels.
2 He is too task-centred and does too much 'fire-fighting'. But remember he lacks 'good' information and is under pressure from the factory manager. However, responsibility for appropriate information and control systems is his. Also failing to manage boundaries of department and to represent its interests with factory manager.
3 *Against*: The factory manager is correct that information will continue to be 'someone else's responsibility'. This is also incongruent with the notion of self-managing groups. *For*: By making the system someone's responsibility, it is possible to ensure change happens quickly since no major education or attitude change is required. On balance the latter is preferred as a temporary measure especially since a successful new system will begin to change people's attitudes to information.
4 Eight criteria were specified. The new system should (i) provide information

consistent with concepts used by operators; (ii) be consistent with and further team-working; (iii) be accurate and have no systematic bias; (iv) be perceived as fair by management and staff; (v) be responsive to events to allow teams to regulate their behaviour; (vi) be simple enough to administer routinely; (vii) be consistent with existing management systems; and (viii) not be too expensive to administer.

5   No, a unitary system is preferable to help create integrated teams. Thus, criterion (ii) takes precedence over (i). Separate systems would institutionalize differences within the teams.

6   A simple system involved two aspects. On a daily basis, the display on a blackboard of the target by product line for each team in batches assuming no scrap. Batch target updated by clerical assistant whenever necessary (for example, as a result of machine breakdown, incidence of scrap, overtime working or absenteeism). Progress against these targets posted systematically (at mid-morning, lunchtime and end of day). On a weekly basis, available on the first day of the following week, a summary sheet showing for each team the revised batch targets, the completed batches, the amount of scrap (in batch equivalents), overall efficiency and, for information only, overall machine utilization. All these activities are the responsibility of the clerical assistant.

7   All became much more aware of the importance of information recording since it led directly to modifications of daily targets (up and down). This led to more discussion with the clerical assistant and a much better understanding of links between targets, efficiency, breakdowns, overtime, scrap and utilization. This process took several months.

   Some conflict was caused for the manager since the clerical assistant in effect was changing targets (for example, by recording a breakdown). It was agreed that this could be done for routine and small stoppages but that major modifications had to be referred to the manager.

   The new system also increased the opportunity for direct managerial control since it provided more accurate and more useful information. If the manager responds by tightening controls on a team, in effect eroding their new discretionary areas, conflict will result.

8   Production planning – was required to plan further ahead to even out production requirements, so as to keep the teams intact; it made their forecasting role harder; led to marginally increased inventory costs; and led to some loss of flexibility in other production departments who could no longer call on operators from the department under examination here.

   Work study – came under some pressure from operators to alter 'unfair' standard times; the standards on some product lines were relaxed and some tightened as a result of informal negotiations.

   Maintenance engineering – came under a lot of pressure from operators in the department under examination to improve service; more accurate recording highlighted and made public the costs of machine downtime; the engineers became more responsive to needs of the department and were approached directly by team members, not just by the manager; the engineers felt they lost some of their own autonomy and freedom of action.

9   *Advantages*: more frequent updates of target and production information are possible; a more sophisticated analysis of efficiency, utilization and productivity is possible; there is the possibility of more direct control (to managers an advantage); in time it could be integrated with systems controlling flow of raw materials, stock levels and market information. *Disadvantages*: the direct cost of new equipment; the cost of educating and training staff; the possibility of more direct visibility and

accountability (to the shop floor a disadvantage). *Overall*: in this situation the benefits did not outweigh the costs.

10 Information is not the same as control though the former can provide opportunities for the latter. Usually there is too much information in organizations and of the wrong kind, in the wrong place and at the wrong time. The key issues focus on who wants what information, aggregated and presented in what way, how often and when. Thus, information systems should be directly relevant to user needs. One problem is that information systems tend to evolve and when they are designed this is often without consultation with the users. Since people in different roles have different needs and since these needs change over time, information systems should work off a common data base but otherwise be very flexible. Integrated systems which cut across functions can be useful in promoting integration within organizations, particularly those facing high levels of uncertainty (see Galbraith 1973).

References and Further Reading

Clegg C W Fitter M J (1978) Information systems: the Achilles heel of job redesign? Personnel Review, 7: 5–11

Fitter M J (1982) Information systems and the organisational implications of job redesign, in Autonomy and Control at the Workplace, edited by J E Kelly and C W Clegg, Croom Helm

Galbraith J (1973) Designing Complex Organizations, Addison-Wesley

Hackman J R Oldham G R (1976) Motivation through the design of work: test of a theory, Organizational Behavior and Human Performance, 15: 250–279

Miner J B (1982) Theories of Organizational Structure and Process, Dryden Press

Oldham G R Hackman J R (1980) Work design in the organizational context, in Research in Organizational Behavior, Vol. 2, edited by B M Staw and L L Cummings, JAI Press

Sime M E Coombs M J (eds) (1983) Designing for Human–Computer Communication, Academic Press

Tricker R I (1976) Management Information and Control Systems, John Wiley

CASE 7 Decision Making: British Rail
Riccardo Peccei and David Guest

Theoretical Background

The Nature of Decision Making
Should the focus be on decision taking at a single point or on a process? The case can be seen either as a set of decisions or as a continuous process in the form of a recurring cycle (Mintzberg et al. 1976).

Decision Making as a Facet of Organizational Life
Should decision making be viewed as a rational exercise among managers with a community of interest or a compromise among vested interests? Key ideas or themes include intra-organizational conflict – uncertainty, differentiation, integration, differences in objectives (Lawrence and Lorsch 1967); muddling through (Lindblom 1959); 'garbage can' models of decision making (Cohen et al. 1972); task uncertainty and decision making – uncertainty reduction, project management, organic forms of organization (Galbraith 1977).

Strategies of Change

Decision implementation will be linked to the view of organizational life held by key actors: rational view → rational empirical strategy (e.g. persuasion, training); conflict view → power-coercive (e.g. imposition, 'buying-out') or a normative–re-educative strategy (e.g. T-groups, counselling). (See Chin and Benne 1976.)

Bureaucracy

The main characteristics include the division of labour, vertical and horizontal job specialization, formalization of rules, procedures and behaviour, hierarchy of authority, chain of command, regulated communication, standardization of work processes and skills. The case illustrates the complexities of change in large organizations and the operation of the 'bureaucratic phenomenon'. (Key themes include unclear accountability, blockages to progress, vicious circle of control, problem of highly formalized and centralized decision-making processes, rule-boundedness and lack of flexibility and adaptability.) (See Child 1984.)

Although the case is pitched mainly at the organizational level, any wider analysis also needs to consider individual and group decision making (e.g. 'rational man', information processing – selection, overload; attitude change/consistency; group processes and intergroup behaviour – 'group think', polarization of decisions by groups or committees), i.e. social and cognitive influences on decision making. (See Morley and Hoskin 1984.)

What Actually Happened

The management decided to press ahead with the existing scheme. Work on the RCT scheme was resumed in mid-1979 after management got ASLEF agreement to the Eggborough trials as part of BR's May 1979 national pay and productivity settlement. However, before the trials could start the lineside equipment at Eggborough had to be overhauled and the two Class 56 locomotives had to be fitted with RCT equipment. This work was not completed until early 1981. At the same time management sought permission from the unions to proceed with site work at the other two power stations with a view to extending the trials to the other two locations. The unions, however, refused to consider any extension of the trials until those at Eggborough had been completed and the results fully discussed and evaluated. Prior to starting the trials a new investment submission had to be prepared for the project since the previous authorization had expired. The new target date for the completion of the evaluation trials was set for November 1981, and that for the full operational commissioning of the scheme for January 1984. The new investment submission was approved in early 1981 and a year later, when the data for the present case study were collected, evaluation trials of the RCT system were successfully completed at Eggborough. As far as the authors are aware, however, the unions have not yet agreed to the principle of remote control and the RCT scheme has not yet been introduced at the three power stations.

Answers

1 Having overcome the technical problems, and taking into account the possible extension of the scheme to other power stations, (b) is now the most sensible. (a) might be easiest, but evades the underlying industrial relations issues. (c) could have been tried earlier, buying in the foreign version, but it is too late now.

2 With hindsight, the Research Department and the CMEE Department were over-

ambitious in their claims, partly as a result of attempts to establish themselves within BR. It would have been quicker and probably cheaper to buy in the tried and tested foreign system. Arguably the case denies the existence of a single key decision. In practice, the decision to allow the Research Department to develop a system instead of using the foreign one was a major cause of the subsequent problems.

3   Three types of factors caused delays at various times: (i) technical problems (under-estimating development difficulties; over-optimistic target dates; failure to integrate with other schemes; failure to adopt new remote control technology); (ii) organizational problems (centralized, complex decision-making and authorization process; decisions taken in the absence of an understanding of the nature of the project; inadequate interdepartmental coordination; divorce of technical and managerial responsibilities; problems of commitment and continuity when delays mean staff changes and departmental reorganizations are taking place); (iii) industrial relations problems (resistance by ASLEF; failure by management to prevent protracted consultation).

4   Industrial relations within BR reflected the bureaucratic structure. The processes of negotiation and consultation were therefore complex and slow and normally handled by specialists within the Industrial Relations Department. Specifically this resulted in the absence of an agreed strategy towards the unions, an emphasis on caution, and a failure to develop a sense of urgency, for example by setting deadlines for the consultation process. In practice, although it is tempting to seek scapegoats, the unions were not the only nor necessarily the main source of delay. For the future more emphasis on decentralization of certain industrial relations issues, greater clarity of industrial relations objectives in relation to other organizational objectives, and less concern to seek an accommodation for its own sake should be considered.

5   Arguably any evaluation should take account of: (i) the context and the resources available; (ii) a cost–benefit analysis, including some assessment of management time; (iii) the subjective evaluations of stake-holders; (iv) an analysis of the actual process, through departments, committees, etc. This implies an evaluation of *process* and *outcomes*.

6   BR's systems of authorization sought to impose rationality. In some cases this helped to ensure that a sound decision was made, but often at the cost of considerable delays in the decision-making process. The problem with rational decision making lies in the concept of rationality and the question of *whose* rationality? Thus ASLEF and the Research Department may have behaved rationally from their own perspectives, if not from that of BR Headquarters.

7   Large organizations must find ways of becoming less subject to the bureaucratic phenomenon. As a first step this means identifying smaller, manageable units and appointing managers with full authority (BR have now introduced a system of sector managment to achieve this – see Burgoyne 1985). Specific projects will benefit from a project manager with sufficient authority to progress the project. With major initiatives or decisions in bureaucracies taking a long time to develop and implement, turnover of key staff (including those on project team) can be a problem. Effective information systems and sensible career planning can help to ensure continuity on long-term projects. A central lesson is that bureaucratic structures can easily delay decision making but very seldom accelerate it.

References and Further Reading

Burgoyne J (1985) Management development: British Rail, in Case studies in Organizational Behaviour, edited by C W Clegg, N J Kemp and K Legge, Harper & Row, Case 17

Child J (1984) Organization: A Guide to Problems and Practice, 2nd edition, Harper & Row

Chin R Benne K D (1976) General strategies for affecting changes in human systems, in The Planning of Change, edited by W G Bennis, K D Benne, R Chin and K E Corley, Holt, Rinehart & Winston

Cohen M D March J G Olsen J P (1972) A garbage can model of organizational choice, Administrative Science Quarterly 17: 1–25

Dodgson J S (1983) British Rail after Serpell, Three Banks Review, Autumn, pp. 22–37

Galbraith J (1977) Organization Design, Addison-Wesley

Lawrence P R Lorsch J W (1967) Organization and Environment: Managing Differentiation and Integration, Harvard Graduate School of Business Administration

Lindblom C E (1959) The science of muddling through, Public Administration Review, 19: 79–88

Mintzberg H Raisingham D Theoret A (1976) The structure of 'unstructured' decision processes, Administrative Science Quarterly, 21: 246–275

Morley I E Hoskin D M (1984) Decision-making and negotiation, in Social Psychology and Organizational Behaviour, edited by M Gruneberg and T Wall, John Wiley

CASE 8   Power and Politics: TVN
Iain Mangham

Theoretical Background

This includes (a) political theory of organizations (see, for review, Pfeffer 1981); (b) interactionist perspectives on organization (see Mangham 1985; Strauss 1978; Hewitt 1984); and network theory (see Tichy et al. 1979). The various political theories view organizations as pluralistic, divided into interests, subcultures, competing individuals and coalitions, and regard action as the resultant of struggle, bargaining and compromise (not necessarily initially desired by either party).

The source of power in organizations is often argued to be the ability of a particular member to deliver some valued resource or performance and the inability of others to derive that resource or performance from elsewhere. Thus, in the present case, Neville Cottingham may be seen as the cost-cutting, organizing resource and Tony Dancer the person who supplies the creative energy. Neville Cottingham's skill, of course, may be the ability to cope with what are taken to be important organizational problems ('sorting the organization out') and as such may be highly valued by the Board. There is evidence that control of key resources is an important element of power (see Crozier 1964; Hinings et al. 1974). There is also evidence to suggest that powerful people vary in their manner of influencing others (see Patchen 1974; Mowday 1978; Kipnis et al. 1980).

What Actually Happened

Neville Cottingham talked to his Chairman and persuaded him that Dancer's skills were such that he would be the ideal man to head up a new subsidiary which would produce films for TVN. He was careful to sound out potential successors to Dancer in his role as Director of Programmes and to check his moves with the IBA before he spoke to the Chairman. Having lined up the parties (the IBA, the Board, and good candidates), he spoke to Dancer offering him the position of managing director of the new subsidiary. Dancer, clearly much more interested in what he termed 'creative activity' than in administration, saw an opportunity to escape the controls being imposed upon him and accepted with alacrity. Thus TVN retained the services of both men.

Using his ideas about power and politics in organizations, Cottingham formed a strong alliance with his new Director of Programmes (his appointment, of course, thus creating a degree of obligation) and began the drive for efficiency in that area, using a newly constituted Budget and Programme Committee consisting of senior programme makers, accountants, operations personnel and himself in the chair.

Answers

1 It is important that, in attempting to answer the questions, students try to put themselves into the situation. In particular, they should recognize that the exercise of power and the conflict it engenders may well create considerable emotion.

The range of questions may, of course, be wide, but should include the following: (i) What has just happened to me? (I have been made to look silly in front of other executives? I have demanded information and been refused it – again very publicly.) (ii) Is what has just happened an isolated event or is it the culmination of a series of things? (iii) What does such behaviour imply for (a) my reputation, (b) my sense of well being (Can I take much more of this?) and (c) my ability to render the organization more efficient and effective?

The aim of such questions is to assess some of the feelings and some of the perceptions Neville Cottingham has at the moment the meeting concludes. If he is, for example, angry or hurt, feels he has lost and been made a fool of, he needs to be aware of such emotions *in order that* he does not act precipitately. 'Here I am now, extremely angry, humiliated even, but acknowledging all of that, if I am to act in a politic fashion, I must think it all out.'

There are other questions to be asked, such as the following: (i) Given this is a showdown (Is it? Can I let it run on now?), who can deploy what? (ii) What does Dancer control? What does TVN need him for? What are his skills? What support is he likely to have and from where? How quickly can he be replaced? (iii) What do I control? What does TVN need me for? What are my skills? What support do I have and from where? How quickly can I be replaced and by whom? What other opportunities do I have?

2 Neville Cottingham has to identify the key actors and may need help in thinking his strategy through. He will probably ask the advice of Tom Beverley (his confidant and industrial relations director) and needs to talk to others in the industry to determine answers to questions about Dancer's support and reputation and to determine who else could do the job. He also needs to talk to the IBA to determine their attitude to a change in programme director, and to the chairman of the board. The *minimum* political support he can move with is that of the IBA and the Board.

3 He can ignore it and proceed as if nothing has happened. Possibly it would be foolish so to do, since such a public challenge will soon be the subject of gossip and will signal that Cottingham is not in control.

He can fire Dancer (or attempt to) thus, probably, antagonizing the programme department, offending the IBA and creating a considerable impact upon the valuation of the company on the Stock Market.

He can find some means of retaining Dancer's services and of bringing the programme department under control.

4 Appropriate mechanisms can be created for monitoring the budgets and the outcomes of the programme department (budget and programme committee).

Organization and team development efforts can be made to effect more appropriate relations between the various departments (see Mangham 1979; French and Bell 1973).

References and Further Reading

Crozier M (1964) The Bureaucratic Phonomenon, University of Chicago Press

French W L Bell C H (1973) Organization Development, Prentice Hall

Hewitt J P (1984) Self and Society, 3rd edition, Allyn & Bacon

Hinings C R Hickson D J Pennings J M Schneck R E (1974) Structural conditions of intra-organizational power, Administrative Science Quarterly 19: 22–44

Kipnis D Schmidt S Wilkinson I (1980) Interorganizational influence tactics: explorations in getting one's way, Journal of Applied Psychology 65: 440–452

Mangham I L (1979) The Politics of Organizational Change, Associated Business Press

Mangham I L (1985) Power and Performance in Organizations, Blackwell

Mowday R T (1978) The exercise of upward influence in organizations, Administrative Science Quarterly 23: 137–156

Patchen M (1974) The locus and basis of influence on organizational decisions, Organizational Behavior and Human Performance 11: 192–221

Pfeffer J (1981) Power in Organizations, Pitman

Strauss A (1978) Negotiations, Jossey Bass

Tichy N M Tushman M L Fombrun C (1979) Social network analysis for organizations, Academy of Management Review 4: 507–519

CASE 9 Organizational Consulting and Development: John Player and Sons
Roy Payne and Bill Reddin

Theoretical Background

The theoretical ideas behind this case concern (a) creating a coherent environment by involving people, (b) improving interpersonal relationships by unfreezing, changing and refreezing people's beliefs or values about how to behave, (c) developing candour and trust, (d) setting objectives to improve performance by generating knowledge of results and feedback, (e) structuring experiences to get the common language and behaviour the consultant and/or client desires, (f) 'modelling' desirable behaviour for the client and (g) starting from the top down. Running throughout the programme there are cycles of diagnosis, solution generation, planning, acting and evaluating. This is done for individuals, teams, departments and the organization as a whole. Most texts on organization development (OD) describe the theoretical origins of these ideas (e.g. Beckhard 1969).

What Actually Happened

The programme was completed for all managers over a two and a half year period. The programme was evaluated by the company, the consultant and an external team. All agreed changes had taken place, that the company management was in better shape, though the external evaluators were cautious about just how much had changed, and whether a structured programme of change as used by Reddin was likely to lead to radical change, as opposed to evolutionary change. These competing perspectives on change can be pursued in the literature of Watzlawick et al. (1974), and Argyris (1970).

Answers

1 This is what was covered in the formal contract: (a) objectives of the programme; (b) definition of who would participate in the various stages of the programme, e.g. all managers attend a five-day managerial effectiveness seminar; (c) access to any person or meeting in the company; (d) appointment of an OD manager and an OD adviser selected from within the company by Reddin; (e) establishment of a committee to direct the programme consisting of Reddin, a director to chair it, the OD manager and his assistant and two directors elected by the other directors for the first year – the committee was to operate by consensus, to be responsible for the effectiveness of the programme and accountable to the Board; (f) timetable of major events; (g) roles of Reddin, e.g. to advise and to conduct top team role laboratories and the corporate strategy laboratory; (h) number of consultant days, and costs; (i) facilities allocated to consultants.

2 Reddin chose these elements in designing the organizational effectiveness committee. This is pretty well his standard design.

Item	*Why*
All directors serve on the committee at some time.	To increase their commitment and understanding of the programme.
The committee should have six or seven members.	Reddin believes this to be close to optimum for highly interactive discussion.
The committee should commence with three directors with serving periods of 6, 12, 18 months respectively.	To facilitate rotation and give enough time for learning.
Reddin should not be a committee member.	To facilitate making it their problem not his and to lower any threat his membership might be for some. Reddin observed some meetings but not all and gave his comments freely.
The committee's authority was to discuss any programme innovations or changes put before it by anyone and to agree with them by consensus, or not. Those agreed to by consensus to be put to the Board.	Reddin believes that if you insist on consensus you are more likely to get a better decision and higher commitment.
All items agreed first by consensus by the committee and then agreed by consensus by the full board (this was another condition) to be distributed to all senior managers.	If you are arguing for openness and candour, it becomes necessary to demonstrate it.

3   The internal consultants must be credible in terms of age, appearance (not too 'hairy'), experience and career route; they must have low intrusive personal needs (all the way from whether wanting to be loved or wanting to win or being too ambitious) and a low knowledge of behavioural science (because their role is facilitator not trainer).

4   Reddin has a formal, structured, team-building programme, the Team Role Laboratory (TRL), which is used by consultants around the world in a variety of settings. It was the one used at JP&S and the same programme was used with semiliterate foremen of rural industries in Third World countries: it is used in just the same way with a top team, or bottom team of Fortune 500 companies, in one case a bank employing 35 000 people at many levels.

    The design should be and is composed of: (1) effectiveness areas (objectives) of the team (what are the outputs, what is the team job); (2) effectiveness areas (objectives) of each team member; (3) perceived style of each team member; (4) how each team member can help the other; (5) outstanding problems the team should solve which it could solve if it worked on them; (6) team decision-making practices and how they should be changed; (7) team meeting practices and how they should be changed; (8) team organization structure and how it should be changed; (9) team diagnosis in terms of process – who talks, who listens, how they handle conflict, etc.

5   The objectives could include the following: (a) improved objective setting; (b) increased commitment to managers' objectives; (c) increased commitment to team objectives; (d) increased acceptance of and readiness for change at all levels of management; (e) identifying the need for and facilitating the implementation of change as appropriate; (f) improve interfunctional cooperation; (g) increased use of participation in decision making when this improves the decisions or obtains necessary commitment; (h) increased job satisfaction; (i) increased candour and trust at all levels of management.

6   The 29 senior managers met for a whole day to determine how well the organizational effectiveness programme was meeting the objectives outlined in the previous question. They were divided into four teams and set the tasks of (1) rating progress alone, (2) agreeing progress in the team, and (3) suggesting ways of removing impediments to progress.

    The progress made as agreed by all four teams is listed below:

Objectives	*Progress*
Improved objective setting	Some new things better (e.g. projects, reorganizations, and new jobs)
Increased commitment to managers' objectives	Some but varied (through TRL and team effectiveness conferences which are designed as a follow-up and evaluation of the TRL some months after the TRL has taken place)
Increased commitment to team objectives	Progress made (where appropriate)

Objectives	Progress
Increased acceptance of and readiness for change at all levels of management	Good progress
Identifying the need for and facilitating the implementation of change as appropriate	Good identification – short term almost too good, not so good long term; implementation – slow.
Improve interfunctional cooperation	Good progress
Increased use of participation in decision making when this improves the decisions or obtains necessary commitment	Some – good

7 Table A shows significant changes in mean scores for the main questionnaire measures collected by an independent research team. Note that the two climate scales in Table A showed changes: 'leaders' psychological distance' and 'interpersonal aggression'. The research team's comments on these data in a report to the company were:

'There is a general tendency for individuals to see themselves as more flexible and ready to accept change. Interpersonal relations seem to be better and senior people are seen as more approachable. People seem more satisfied with the people around them (colleagues and subordinates in particular). The main changes have taken place amongst those who are at the lower levels. Both these groups started with less positive attitudes to the company and therefore had the greatest scope for change. Middle and senior managers attitudes have not changed at all but they did start out as relatively positive.'

Table A Summary of differences between T_1, T_2, and T_3 (in cases where we can have confidence at the $P < 0.05$ level or better)

	June 1971	Dec. 1971	Oct. 1972	Confidence	N
The organization as a whole					
Readiness to change	21.0	22.6	23.4	0.01	465
Satisfaction with colleagues	26.1	26.5	27.2	0.05	466
Satisfaction with subordinates	31.2	32.0	33.2	0.05	455
Leaders' psychological distance	3.6	3.3	2.8	0.01	458
Interpersonal aggression	3.1	2.8	2.3	0.05	454

References and Further Reading

Argyris C (1970) Intervention Theory and Method, Addison-Wesley
Argyris C Schön D (1974) Improving Professional Practice, Jossey-Bass
Beckhard R (1969) Organization Development Strategies and Models, Addison-Wesley
Blake R Mouton J S (1964) The Managerial Grid, Gulf Publishing
Bowers D W (1973) OD techniques and their results in 23 organizations, Journal of Applied Behavioral Science, 9: 21–43
Clark P A (1972) Organizational Design: Theory and Practice, Tavistock
Golembiewski R T (1979) Approaches to Planned Change Part II: Macro-level Interventions and Change Agent Strategies, University of Georgia Press

Lawrence P Lorsch J (1967) Organization and Environment, Harvard Business School
Legge K (1984) Evaluating Planned Organizational Change, Academic Press
Mintzberg H (1979) The Structuring of Organizations, Prentice-Hall
Mirvis P Berg D (1977) Failures in Organization Development and Change, John Wiley
Porras J L Berg P O (1978) The impact of organization development, Academy of Management
    Review, 3: 249–266
Reddin W J (1970) Managerial Effectiveness, McGraw-Hill
Reddin W J (1971) Effective Management by Objectives, Business Publications
Reddin W J (1975) Every manager's clear responsibility, Management in Action, January
Reddin W J (1978) A consultant confesses, Management Today, January
Spooner P (1973) Players assesses the value of its OD shake-up, in Business Administration, 1973,
    pp. 362–365
Watzlawick P Weakland J Fisch R (1974) Change: Principles of Problem Formation and Problem
    Resolution, W W Norton

CASE 10   Small Businesses: Family Firms and Management – J & S Nicholson Ltd
Robert Goffee and Richard Scase

Theoretical Background

The characteristics of small businesses include flexibility, informality (work tasks and procedures are not precisely specified, adjustment of work roles according to task at hand) and a 'team' or 'family' atmosphere. Such 'organic' structures are often contrasted with mechanistic structures which involve detailed job descriptions, clearly specified rules and procedures, and the coordination of work tasks through hierarchical systems of decision making (Burns and Stalker 1961). Organic structures are linked with motivation, job satisfaction and high trust relations (Fox 1974), but can contain latent control mechanisms which allow proprietors to retain control over their businesses despite allowing managerial autonomy (Goffee and Scase 1985). The organic form allows discretion in conditions of uncertainty (Crozier 1964) and so is suitable for firms in the building industry (Tavistock Institute of Human Relations 1976; Foster 1969). 'Quasi-organic' structures (informal but involving a *limited* decentralization) allow delegation without diminishing owner-control. In Mintzberg's terms, the organization is a hybrid which displays the flexibility of the 'simple structure', the decentralization of the 'professional bureaucracy' and the output standardization of the 'divisionalized form' (Mintzberg 1979).

What Actually Happened

After lengthy consultations with his brother, Jim Nicholson personally took over the chairmanship of interior fittings in 1983. Steven Nicholson retained his ownership stake and directorship on the board of the holding company. Steven's main responsibilities became public relations. Graham Jackson renewed his productive relationship with Jim Nicholson and decided to remain with the company. However, the situation altered dramatically early in 1984. After brief consultations with his brother and financial director, Graham Sharpe, Jim Nicholson announced his resignation as managing director and the appointment to this position of a highly qualified and experienced 38 year old man, Simon Walters, who had worked previously with a national contractor. Walter's recruitment had been handled by a management recruitment agency and came as a complete surprise to senior management within Nicholsons. The new man immediately set about 'tightening up' financial and procedural controls over the construction and interior fitting subsidiaries. Alan Pearson interpreted this as a threat to his own position and to the future of construction. Graham Jackson was initially disturbed by the lack of consultation over Walter's appointment and later unhappy about the implications for his own future in Nicholsons. As a result Pearson began looking for positions elsewhere and Jackson started to reconsider the option of starting his own business.

Answers

1 The major problems facing Jim Nicholson were related to (a) the future shape and direction of the business; (b) his own role and that of his brother, Steven; (c) the career aspirations of the subsidiary managing directors and (d) his eventual successor as managing director of the holding company.

2 Jim Nicholson's managerial style is based upon a strong personality, sound technical knowledge and a distrust of rules, regulations and procedures. In the early days this encouraged him to 'lead by example' – an appropriate strategy for a 'small employer' (Goffee and Scase 1982). Later, the style remained applicable to Reg Walker and the small works subsidiary. But it limited Alan Pearson's opportunities at construction to take his own initiatives. Graham Jackson benefited from Jim Nicholson's approach: he was given autonomy and the chance to take initiatives. But this was later jeopardized by Jim Nicholson's mistaken and probably ill-considered assumption that his brother could, under instruction, establish a similar relationship with Jackson. As a result of Jim Nicholson's style, then, Walker, Pearson and Jackson were unable to develop the experience necessary for their possible promotion. Rather like his brother Steven, they had all, to a greater or lesser extent, become dependent on Jim.

3 When he joined the business Steven Nicholson brought experience, contacts, administrative ability and funds. From Jim's point of view he was 'trustworthy' because of the family tie. However, such directors brought in some time after start up are often less motivated than the founders and their entry frequently solves a short-term difficulty at the expense of a long-term problem, as in this case.

4 The holding company and subsidiary structure facilitates owner-delegation but the autonomy gained by senior managers is of a kind that can be closely monitored and measured. Arbitrary interventions by proprietors are also faciliated. (See 'Theoretical Background' above.) As a result, the development of senior managerial staff can be seriously impeded and the succession of owners may precipitate a crisis.

5 (See 'What Actually Happened' above.) Separating Steven Nicholson and Graham Jackson appears an appropriate strategy – with both subsequently able to specialize in areas of strength. The short-term 'cost' is yet another demanding role for Jim Nicholson. Owner-managers often 're-appear' to solve problems precisely when they are intending to withdraw (Gorb 1981).

6 Jim Nicholson finds himself on the horns of a dilemma, from which there is no easy escape. As a result of managerial style and organizational structure no appropriate internal successors have been developed. An internal appointment is therefore risky. But bringing in an 'outsider' threatens the 'family ethos' of the firm and the motivation and commitment of senior managerial staff.

7 The present structure helps to (a) spread financial risks; (b) specify cost centres; (c) monitor outputs (in an industry where the work process itself is difficult to measure); (d) relate specialized expertise to distinct products; (e) encourage market

responsiveness; (f) enable proprietors to assess managerial effectiveness (Mintzberg 1979, Chap. 20). However, when combined with the managerial style of family firm proprietors this structure can lead to (a) destructive internal competition; (b) poor communications; (c) a lack of management development amongst senior managerial staff. A restructuring along functional lines is inappropriate given the complex work processes and market uncertainty of the construction industry. A feature of family-owned businesses is the reluctance of founder-proprietors to delegate decision making and give attention to management succession. Future viability of the business is dependent on Jim Nicholson withdrawing from management and devoting greater attention to management training and development. Further, in the competitive environment of the 1980s, it may be desirable for the company to concentrate upon the growth area of interior fitting.

References and Further Reading

Burns T Stalker G (1961) The Management of Innovation, Tavistock
Crozier M (1964) The Bureaucratic Phenomenon, Tavistock
Foster C (1969) Building with Men, Tavistock
Fox A (1974) Beyond Contract: Work, Power and Trust Relations, Faber and Faber
Goffee R Scase R (1982) Fraternalism and paternalism as employer strategies in small firms, in Diversity and Decomposition in the Labour Market, edited by G Day, Gower
Goffee R Scase R (1985) Proprietorial control in family firms: some functions of quasi-organic management systems, Journal of Management Studies 22: 53–68
Gorb P (ed.) (1981) Small Business Perspectives, Armstrong Publishing
Mintzberg H (1979) The Structuring of Organisations, Prentice-Hall
Tavistock Institute of Human Relations (1976) Interdependence and Uncertainty: A Study of the Building Industry, Tavistock

CASE 11   Organizational Structure: Gamma Appliances
Andrew Kakabadse

Theoretical Background

To analyse a structure, three factors must be taken into account. These factors are interdependent and in combination provide the organization with its shape, culture and identity. A total organizational perspective should be adopted (Kakabadse et al. 1985, Chap. 9)

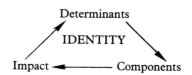

Determinants are those factors which have determined the present culture and structure of the organization; technology, size, ownership, external environment, history of the organization, financial performance, geographic location and dispersion, and the people and their attitudes (see Child 1984; Mintzberg 1979).

Components are those elements of structure such as organization charts or role hierarchies and decision making patterns. The questions that need to be analysed are:

(a) is the organization structured according to a production, functional, divisional or matrix structure; (b) is it possible to distinguish a pattern of decision making; (c) within existing structures, how is information transmitted throughout the organization? By analysing these questions, it is possible to identify whether a new structure is required.

In combination, these factors make an *impact* on the organization. Two areas in particular are affected: the span of accountability, and the culture of the organization.

The span of accountability refers to the number of people that any one manager is accountable for, i.e. the overall structure that the manager controls. Changing the structure may increase or decrease the size of the department or unit or division for which each manager is held accountable. The likely response of each manager (stakeholder) affected by reorganization, needs to be taken into account. One or more powerful stakeholders who oppose the reorganization, could prevent it from taking place.

As a result of changes in structure, the culture (i.e. shared norms, attitudes and deemed acceptable ways of behaviour) is likely to alter. A tall hierarchy, with limited spans of managerial control, is likely to stimulate a formal, controlling leadership style among the managers. Equally, the employees may feel that their degree of challenge and responsibility is limited. Yet, for those that find such a culture acceptable, the degree of identification with the organization may be high. People keep to the existing rules and systems and may genuinely direct their loyalty to the organization rather than to their group or to particular individuals.

In a matrix structure, people may adopt different attitudes. They may feel the degree of challenge and responsibility in their jobs is high, and as a result, the quantity and quality of work completed is equally high. The leadership styles need to be more open, informal and confronting, but that is largely due to the fact that managers cannot rely solely on the formal authority to get people to complete tasks. In a matrix structure, individuals interact with many people by holding membership in various teams and possibly by changing jobs regularly. People are unlikely to tolerate an authoritarian style of management. Managers have to use their interpersonal skills to influence their bosses, colleagues and subordinates. (See Galbraith 1977; Lawrence and Lorsch 1967.)

What Actually Happened

Gamma followed Tim Edwards' advice and reorganized Business Services using a matrix structure. Redundancies occurred. Extensive training and team development took place. Felix Benjamin left Gamma. For more details, see 'Answers'.

Answers

1 The main problems were neatly summarized by Edwards in his presentation to the Board members. These include: interpersonal problems and demoralization; an inadequate management information system (MIS); and operational problems such as poor servicing and unavailability of parts. *Note*: these can be seen as symptoms. Core problem is that the present functional structure has become a hindrance to Gamma operations. It is too centralized, and promotes differentiation and rivalry rather than integration. The main problems then are of organizational structure and of how to manage change.

2 Yes – reorganize business services. Develop a matrix structure (see Fig. A) and create regional teams of experts to support customers in the sales, maintenance, spare parts and finance areas. By working closer together, a far more integrated service can be provided to attend to customer needs.

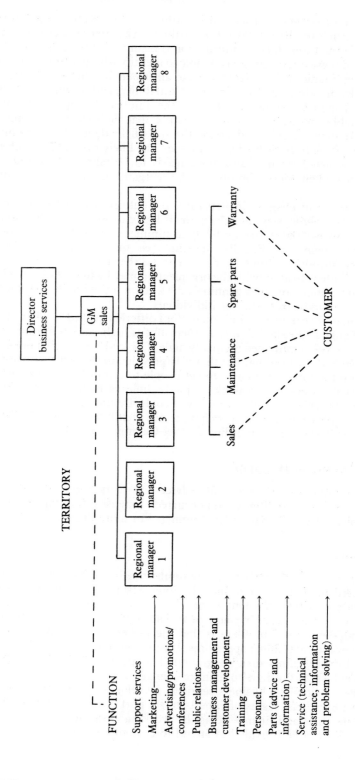

Figure A Matrix organization

The matrix structure can also help to break down some of the old rivalries and interdepartmental jealousies, especially between marketing and sales, by forming two departments to work together, through a shared MIS. Reorganizing structures also gives senior management a mechanism for identifying those jobs required to achieve the aims of business operations, and hence those which are no longer necessary.

Further, the reorganized structure addresses the low morale problem. Regional managers become the new centres of power. By ensuring that the new regional teams are given the authority to respond to regional needs, it is possible to provide individuals with greater control over their jobs in the short and medium term.

3   *Arguments for new structure*   Management information systems (MIS) – the company does not have sufficient information concerning sales or demand for after-sales service, throughout the UK. A more market-sensitive structure will mean one person is held accountable for collating all necessary information and then passing it on for others to process and introduce into the strategic planning process.

People and their attitudes – the employees in Gamma are demoralized. Redundancies have occurred, feelings of insecurity are prominent, and little positive direction is offered by top management. The employees were not prepared for market changes and hence unprepared for the ensuing organizational decline. It is vital that policies be implemented with which people can identify, after the trauma of redundancies and substantial changes.

Arguments against new structure   It is potentially too radical a change for Gamma Appliances; middle and top management may not be able to accept devolution of power and authority; managers may not have the skills to work in the new structure; and building integrated teams at the customer interface may take too long or be too expensive.

4   Yes – but from a management viewpoint the issue of redundancies needs handling sensitively. Benjamin's confronting style is inappropriate in this context. In practice he was moved to another part of the parent organization. If possible, Gamma should manage redundancies quickly, offering good terms and using volunteers where possible. (See Case 16 by Stephen Wood.)

5   Making the new structure work depends on being able to develop effective teams at various levels in the hierarchy, i.e. regional teams, directorate teams and support teams in the areas of marketing, spare parts, and warranty. In reality, team development programmes were organized for regional teams, the directorate team and the main board team. In addition, workshops were provided for all managers identifying the benefits, problems and skills required to work in a matrix. The training proved to be beneficial and the managers quickly adapted to their new roles.

The problems in motivating and developing the skills of the managers in part depend on how well the redundancy programme is managed and on how well people are prepared for their new roles.

6   With regard to the strategic relationship with the USA, it is imperative that Gamma becomes more efficient and profitable in order to be able to negotiate on a more equal footing with the USA parent company. The plant in the USA is operating at under capacity. In such a situation it is difficult to predict what decisions will be made concerning constantly under-utilized capital. Gamma needs to demonstrate that it can function as a profitable and independent enterprise, because as far as strategic decision making is concerned, the company is in a vulnerable position. The Americans may decide to close down the UK manufacturing operation rather than sacrifice their USA plant.

References and Further Reading

Kakabadse A P Ludlow R Vinnicombe S (1985) Working in Organizations, Gower (in press)

Kakabadse A P (1983) Politics of Management, Gower

Newman H Warner E K Schnel J E (1982) The Process of Management: Strategy, Action, Results, 5th edition, Prentice-Hall

Galbraith J R (1977) Organization Design, Addison-Wesley

Lawrence P R Lorsch J W (1976) Organization and Environment, Harvard University Press

Mintzberg H (1979) The Structuring of Organizations, Prentice-Hall

Child J (1984) Organizations: A Guide to Problems and Practice, 2nd edition, Harper & Row

SECTION 2: Personnel Management

CASE 12　Absence and Turnover: The Absentee Bus Crews
Nigel Nicholson

Theoretical Background

Despite its compendious size and long history, the absence research literature yields few simple answers or reliable generalizations about its causes and conditions. At the individual level, studies have tried to relate absence to such variables as work attitudes, biographical factors, hours of work and job conditions, and at the group level to such factors as organization size, turnover, unemployment and strikes (see Chadwick-Jones et al. 1973; Muchinsky 1977 for reviews of the literature). Strong relationships are periodically to be found but they prove to be unreliable (biographical variables are the most consistent predictors). The response of theorists to this state of affairs has been to concentrate on general process models rather than content specific theories (see, for example, Gibson 1966; Nicholson 1977; Steers and Rhodes 1978).

　Various reasons have been offered for the inconclusive state of knowledge about absence (see Johns and Nicholson 1983 for a critique of predominant approaches), though the most general of these is the fact that absence is a highly complex phenomenon. Indeed, one may doubt the wisdom of regarding it as a single behaviour at all, so varied and contingent are the psychological states, job conditions and environmental contexts that can provoke or inhibit it. Certainly, blanket terms such as 'withdrawal' unhelpfully take us in the wrong direction by creating the illusion of conceptual unity and suggesting invariant linkages with quite different behaviours. The notion of organizational culture in general and 'absence culture' in particular may be more helpful, in suggesting how absence causes may be activated or limited by the surrounding circumstances (Nicholson and Johns 1985).

What Actually Happened

Because the investigation in the Coal Valley Bus Company was only one small part of a large scale multicompany study, there was no scope for an action-research follow up. The main results and summaries of findings, comparing the company with others in the sample, were reported back, but there was no momentum for change and in the long run the study had little impact on the organization. What changes did take place were in piecemeal fashion over the years that followed – the extension of one-man operation to cover more routes and duties being the most significant.

What Might Have Happened – How the Study Could Have Become a Change Intervention

The case material could have formed the basis for an action plan for management. Students writing a consultancy report on the case should first aim to unfreeze existing practices by analysing the current costs to the company, employees and community (see question 1 below). Second, changes can be suggested in most of the areas under questions 2–10 below, especially in work organization, conditions, and management control strategies. These should be approached carefully and cooperatively in a potentially conflictual culture like this. Immediately, management should improve their information systems about absence and manning and set up an absence action committee or working party (ensuring full union participation and support) to raise consciousness and maintain commitment to change. A successful programme of this kind will shift the absence culture to a new basis of mutual responsibility and tangible gains for employees. The experience of cooperative participation in the change programme would also have a favourable impact on the wider organizational culture and intergroup relations.

Answers

1 Direct costs include the costs of a generous sick-pay scheme, over-manning, additional overtime payments, and management time and administration to maintain cover, discipline employees, and run the morning 'taxi' service. Indirect costs are less tangible but no less important: disruptions to services, effects on working relationships, pressure on inspectors and managers. Note that different types of absence (frequent short spell absence versus infrequent long duration absence) have different costs.

2 The regional culture must be well understood and kept in mind in any change programme, but without being significantly alterable by company initiative. However, organizational cultures 'import' and transform values and beliefs from the wider social milieu, and thus their local 'currency' may be modifiable. The issue of perceived legitimacy of absence is a crucial value to consider here.

3 The organizational culture is marked by intergroup conflict, status differentiation, fragmented work relations, alienation from senior management, union solidarity, and various norms and beliefs about absence. Change can proceed from three sources: (1) structural change in working arrangements which break down divisions and increase cooperation; (2) symbolic initiatives that generate new sentiments and beliefs (such as new communication practices, promoting new images of the company and its service to the community); and (3) new management control strategies which change the role of absence and lateness in the 'psychological contract' with employees.

4 Three relationships are visible between absence and satisfaction: a direct relationship at the intergroup level (comparing drivers and conductors, or the Coal Valley Company with others); an inverse relationship (within the conductors group); and a null relationship (within the drivers group). Students should note how this illustrates the dangers of generalizing about absence–satisfaction relationships without taking account of level of analysis or the surrounding culture. In some cultures absence may be an expression of dissatisfaction, but not in others.

5 Relationships of varying strength are observable here, though, in accordance with the literature, absence is generally inversely related to age and length of service. Students should consider how this may be mediated by differences in workers' lifestyles, domestic responsibilities, central life values, organizational commitment, and financial constraints. It may also be noted that different types of absence may be related to these variables across the different groups.

6 Some connections are implied in the case. Amongst shiftworkers or workers under financial penalties for lateness, absence may be a form of 'lateness conversion'. Turnover is low, but higher in the high absence population of conductors than among drivers. However, it would be ill-advised to lump these together as 'with-

drawal' behaviours for three reasons: (1) not all instances are motivated as voluntary acts of withdrawal; (2) major individual differences are usual in propensity towards each behaviour (e.g. between 'owls' and 'larks' among shiftworkers); (3) they are behaviours at different levels of analysis, and are susceptible to influence by quite different conditions and events.

7 The current rosta system is mechanistic and divisive. Preferable would be a modified regular man system which created team spirit, offered scope for some choice over shifts, duties, partners and overtime, and could form the basis for some performance incentive scheme. Crewmen's resistance to changes could be overcome by experimental introduction of new arrangements, high participation in their determination, and material benefits from their operation and cost-saving. Open recruitment to all grades would offer greater scope for judicious allocation of people to jobs and duties, in particular to buffer individuals who suffer job stresses the most. One-man operation should be extended on routes agreed to be light. The shift system should be examined cooperatively with crewmen to evolve a more flexible pattern of duties. Rather than sharing the misery of bad duties and disliked shifts, a more patterned system in which inequities have compensatory rewards would allow for better self-selection to jobs and active management strategies of personnel placement.

8 These issues cannot be considered in isolation from those under question 7. Students should note the connections. The environmental working conditions of bus operation and dealing with the public are not fundamentally alterable, though changes in duties and hours would constitute major changes to busmen's job conditions. Pay incentives should be introduced at a level sufficient to differentiate jobs and conditions and to have some real incentive value, but not to a level where they are the major component of the wage packet. Preventive and remedial action may be taken to help busmen counter the stresses and hazards of their work (e.g. health education). The 'taxi service' cannot be allowed to continue as an 'indulgency pattern'. If the need for it is not removed by changes that are implemented, it should be institutionalized as a bus service for busmen who have transportation difficulties for the first shift.

9 Records should be used more effectively to monitor the situation and provide the basis for systematic and regular feedback to employees about individual and group performance. Absence and lateness by permission should be encouraged, and indeed could be used as incentive payments for good performance (i.e. give workers a day off as reward for regular attendance). Other incentives should also be considered, e.g. financial payments, overtime opportunities, the chance to opt for certain favourable duties, etc. Organizational changes described above should be linked with a fresh approach to recruitment, training and placement; improving person–job fit where possible. Inspectors should be trained to be more involved in the process of control, as administrators of feedback to employees and the upward communication of their needs, but counselling and disciplinary functions should be operated at a distance by management so that they do not disturb supervisory relations. Self-certification should be considered, to put absence legislation back where it belongs in the context of management–worker relations, but this would require careful monitoring and control to avoid abuse.

10 The researcher would find it useful to know about family income and the effects on attendance of having wage-earning spouses. More information is also needed on the medical causes of absence, so that absence attributable to chronic, stress-related and transient ailments can be quantified. This would help the assessment of the minimum achievable absence level for this population. Management need to

know more about individual differences in the workforce – in terms of their attitudes, needs, preferences and circumstances – so that a more individualized and planned approach to absence control and manning can be implemented.

References and Further Reading
Chadwick-Jones J K Brown C A Nicholson N (1973). Absence from work: its meaning, measurement and control, International Review of Applied Psychology, 22: 137–156

Gibson J O (1966) Toward a conceptualization of absence behavior of personnel in organizations, Administrative Science Quarterly, 12: 107–133

Johns G Nicholson N (1983) The meanings of absence: new strategies for theory and research, in Research in Organizational Behaviour edited by B M Staw and L L Cummings, Vol. 4, JAI Press, pp. 127–172

Muchinsky P M (1977) Employee absenteeism: a review of the literature, Journal of Vocational Behavior, 10: 316–340

Nicholson N (1977) Absence behaviour and attendance motivation: a conceptual synthesis, Journal of Management Studies, 41: 231–252

Nicholson N Johns G (1985) The absence culture and the psychological contract: who's in control of absence? Academy of Management Review (In press)

Steers R M Rhodes S R (1978) Major influences on employee attendance: a process model, Journal of Applied Psychology 63: 391–407

CASE 13   Selection and Recruitment: HAL
Chris Brotherton

Theoretical Background

A number of issues are raised: (i) psychometric testing, including concepts of validity, reliability and sensitivity (see Cronbach 1970; Landy and Trumbo 1980); (ii) recruitment procedures, including interviewing (see Ungerson 1975, especially Chapters 4–7, 9–10, 12 and 24); (iii) discrimination against women and minority groups (see Runnymede Trust 1980; Ungerson 1975, Chapter 26); (iv) wider personnel issues concerned with appraisal, career progression and management development (see Anstey et al. 1976).

Answers

1   Symptoms of problems include: the complexity of the system, the high cost of the system, the high refusal rate by graduates, the high turnover rate of intake. Underlying this there are a number of procedural and technical problems. *Procedurally*, for example, there is no evidence that jobs have been analysed for skills content; that care has been taken to select and recruit separately for sales management and technical jobs; that any individual is responsible for graduate selection; or that people are trained in how to select (e.g. assess application forms, interview candidates, etc.). HAL is aware that it is projecting an image to potential employees in its method of recruiting; HAL is trying to develop and keep its graduate intake; exit interviews are used to find out reasons for leaving.

   Technical problems exist with the criteria and the predictors (see below).

2   Measures are generally insensitive and unreliable (e.g. superior rating). It is probable that people are not trained in how to assess and rate – it should be recognized that this can be very demotivating, especially for bright newcomers. There is a problem

in that personnel and finance are following different objectives on pay. Personnel staff must strive to maintain differentials if they wish to keep good recruits. The company should also distinguish between training for programming and for management – it is the latter that is important. There is a need to look at promotion prospects – is there a need for a 'fast track'? The company must also look closely at turnover and find out why it occurs. Making 20% of graduate recruits from year A redundant was probably a mistake as it will deter future applicants.

3 Interview assessments are important, but using nine sub-scales almost certainly adds nothing. There is a need for specialists here. The company should drop 'assessments' by a graduate host – but maintain the host role for giving information and initial socialization. Psychometric tests should be simplifed – find a modern, single test? The leadership exercise should be dropped.

4 Unintentional discrimination can arise through lack of job analysis – this can lead to inappropriate tests which do not allow the strengths of all candidates to be revealed. Also unintentional bias can be introduced during initial screening or in later interviews. There is a need to ask how many women, for example, are applying? If this is a disproportionately small number, why? Is the wrong image given in publicity? What proportion of those applying are offered jobs? Why? Finally, are some groups leaving at differential rates?

A careful examination of existing data is needed. The company may then need to review publicity, application forms, procedures, etc. There is probably a need to undertake training of people involved in selection.

5 Start again! Any new system should be simple, involve a small group of trained people, be based on requirements of the jobs (different for sales and technical jobs) and be the responsibility of a professional manager in the personnel function (recruit if necessary). Remember, the selection systems create an image with potential employees and need tying-in with subsequent aspects of career progression, management appraisal and development, etc. Advantages of the new approach will be a professionally managed system which should reduce refusals, and could reduce subsequent turnover. But turnover will be reduced only if other changes are made in HAL (career progression, etc.). The disadvantage is that direct costs of the new system will appear higher than before (e.g. higher costs in personnel, especially for training). But the hidden costs will be much lower, a point that has to be forcibly presented to the board if the new selection and recruitment policy is to be adopted.

6 Drop all three psychometric tests. Use an appropriate intelligence test, or a modern 'test battery', and perhaps an 'in-basket' decision exercise for management groups, or a sales simulation for sales candidates.

7 Annual monitoring should be made the responsibility of a manager (see answer to question 5). The system should identify a limited number of criteria (e.g. salary or grade, management appraisal and turnover) and of predictors (e.g. interview assessment and intelligence test). The same manager should be responsible for graduate training and development, keeping in touch with recruits personally (on courses, through appraisals, etc.). The same manager should follow up dissatisfaction and any resignations, using the information available to fine-tune the process.

References and Further Reading

Anstey E Fletcher C Walker J (1976) Staff Appraisal and Development, George Allen & Unwin
Brotherton C J (1980) Paradigms of selection validation: some comments in the light of British equal opportunities legislation, Journal of Occupational Psychology 53: 73–79

Cronbach L J (1970) Essentials of Psychological Testing, 3rd edition, Harper & Row
Dunnette M D (ed.) (1976) The Handbook of Industrial and Organisational Psychology, Rand-McNally, Chapters 18–20
Guion R M (1965) Personnel Testing, McGraw-Hill
Keenan A (1977) Some relationships between interviewers' personal feelings about candidates and their general evaluation of them, Journal of Occupational Psychology 50: 275–284
Landy F J Trumbo D A (1980) Psychology of Work Behavior, Dorsey Press
The Runnymede Trust/British Psychological Society (1980) Discriminating Fairly, The Runnymede Trust
Ungerson B (ed.) (1975) Recruitment Handbook, Gower
Wingrove J Glendinning R Herriot P (1984) Graduate pre-selection: a research note, Journal of Occupational Psychology 57: 169–171

CASE 14 **Training and Skills: Royal Navy**
Don Wallis

Theoretical Background

Psychological learning theories are relevant to the extent (a controversial issue) that they have much to offer in the way of practical application to industrial and military training. Nowadays interest is centred upon cognitive theories, particularly as applied to problem-solving, rather than classical or operant conditioning models (e.g. Bruner 1961, 1966; Duncan 1981). Theories of instruction, and guidelines for setting up optimal conditions for learning, are equally relevant (e.g. Holding 1969; Wallis et al. 1966; Gagné and Briggs 1974; Stammers and Patrick 1975). Students may benefit from briefing about the considerable divergence between theoretical accounts of management training and 'personal development' techniques ('T groups'; interpersonal and social skills training: Smith 1980; Landy and Trumbo 1980), and those which attempt to explain how vocational skills can best be taught and learned. A very recent approach, with a rather different slant, is the 'learning to learn' paradigm which has been researched within the Manpower Services Commission's youth and adult training scheme (Downs and Perry 1984).

The usual psychological and statistical issues in experimental research design are intimately wrapped up in evaluation studies. Students need to appreciate how applied researchers are constrained by the practical circumstances under which a vocational training organization works. They have to learn how to steer safely between the Scylla of doing nothing, because they can't do it with full rigour, and the Charybis of achieving nothing, because they did it without minimal rigour.

What Actually Happened

This is fully documented in the two journal references (Wallis and Wicks 1963; Wallis 1964) up to the completion of evaluating the new training. Note that something like an 'action research' orientation – what an engineering designer would call a 'trials and development' approach – was implicitly followed. When one training regime proved to be less advantageous than expected, improvements were introduced but still within the overall research design.

The 'integrated PI' system of technical training was accepted by the Navy establishment and applied generally to the electrical and radio mechanic training for just about 10 years. Several thousand men were in fact trained in this way. Some follow-up data on the first 36 classes were published later in a review of the early years of 'training technology' as developed and applied widely in all three British armed forces (Wallis, Duncan and Knight 1966).

Answers

1 It would be distinctly unwise (and perhaps professionally unsound?) to try persuading an organization to embark upon so large-scale a commitment without trying first to demonstrate the *potential* benefits on a small scale. One preliminary question to ask is whether the 'new method', wherever applied, can produce better results than the existing method. Or do things more cheaply.

2 An organization is concerned with costs, both material and manpower. Length of training; and *lowest* limits of ability and pre-knowledge which trainees must have. Psychological criteria include performance levels achieved during and after training; pace of learning; retention; transferability to the intended job; generalizability to other jobs.

3 Examination results, which the organization must reveal. Questionnaires to assess acceptability, with respect to trainees or instructional staff. Results of laboratory practical work may also be informative. Reports on trainee's performance later, when undertaking their technical work at sea, would be helpful; but could be unreliable.

4 Students must not insist on experimental designs which depend upon strict controls and conditions which are invariant or wholly experimenter-controlled. (Are there any?) A design in which the new training is compared under reasonably parallel circumstances with the former or existing methods throughout several replications, is likely to be the best practicable, e.g. a quasi-experimental design (Cook and Campbell 1976); action research; or a qualitative research design. An evaluation has to proceed long enough to counter uninvited 'Hawthorne' effects.

5 Performance at the end of new training will have to be better than after the old system; and unless it shows savings in training time or instructional staff or failure rates which at least off-set the capital costs of installing it, the new training should only be recommended with caution.

6 Weaknesses of the preliminary experiment (Wallis and Wicks 1963) are manifest. They include the use of only one 'exemplar' of conventional teaching against which to pitch the PI instructional courses. Esoteric factors like 'time of day' were not controlled. Students should volunteer their ideas on how they would try to conduct such an exploratory enquiry.

7 Job and organizational redesign is worth exploring as an alternative strategy. Some of its psychological benefits may be difficult to engineer in a strictly hierarchical, disciplined, service. Task analysis has indeed been employed widely in the Navy as a technique associated with job design.

8 Rather less so than in a civilian organization. There could nevertheless be implications for selection standards. And the eventual employers of the technicians at sea are likely to monitor the performance of trainees with a critical eye.

9 Students should be able to compare and contrast the instructional techniques for vocational or technical tasks and skills ('technology of training' approach) with the techniques used for developing social and interpersonal skills (group dynamic methods in sensitivity and attitudes training). (Dunnette 1976; Smith 1980; Landy and Trumbo 1980 are relevant.) Both kinds of training are needed in work organizations.

References and Further Reading

Bruner J S (1961) The art of discovery, Harvard Educational Review, 31: 21–32

Bruner J S (1966) Toward a Theory of Instruction, Harvard University Press

Cook T D Campbell D T (1976) The design and conduct of quasi-experiments and true experiments in field settings, in Handbook of Industrial and Organizational Psychology, edited by M D Dunnette, Rand-McNally

Downs S Perry P (1984) Developing learning skills, Journal of European Industrial Training, 8: 21–26

Duncan K D (1981) Training for fault diagnosis in industrial process plant, in Human Detection and Diagnosis of System Failures, edited by J Rasmussen and W B Rouse, Plenum Publishing

Dunnette M D (1976) Aptitudes, abilities, and skills, in Handbook of Industrial and Organizational Psychology, edited by M D Dunnette, Rand-McNally

Gagné R M Briggs L J (1974) Principles of Industrial Design, Holt, Rinehart and Winston

Holding D H (1969) Principles of Training, Pergamon Press

Landy F J Trumbo D A (1980) Psychology of Work Behavior, Dorsey , Chapters 7 and 9

Smith P B (1980) Group Processes and Personal Change, Harper & Row

Stammers R Patrick J (1975) The Psychology of Training, Methuen

Wallis D (1964) Experiments on use of programmed instruction to increase the productivity of training, Occupational Psychology 3 and 4: 141–159

Wallis D Duncan K D Knight M G (1966) Programmed Instruction in the British Armed Forces: A Report on Research and Development, HMSO

Wallis D Wicks R P (1963) The Royal Navy study, Occupational Psychology, 37: 44–84 (reprinted in Programmed Learning 1: 31–47, 1964

CASE 15 Health and Safety at Work: Texchem
Sandra Dawson

Theoretical Background

Health and safety at work can be analysed using concepts and frameworks derived from organizational analysis and industrial relations. An overall view is given in Dawson et al. (1983). There are four key groups of actors: line management, safety specialists, safety representatives and factory inspectors. Their roles and relationships can be explored in terms of the priorities and interests which derive from their organizational position (see Kotter 1982; Stewart 1982, for managers; Dawson et al. 1984a, for specialists; Beaumont 1983; Glendon and Booth 1982, for representatives; the annual reports of the HSE 1983, for the Inspectorate), and their power (Pfeffer 1981; Legge 1978). Issues of how stated policies get translated into practice, particularly in times of economic recession, are also relevant. The position of safety representatives and safety committees needs to be considered within broad changes which characterize developments in industrial relations and labour legislation in the UK (Brown 1981; Bain 1983; Daniel and Millward 1983). The Act and Regulations come within a period of significant extension of both auxilliary and regulative labour legislation (Kahn-Freund 1977) during which the influence of trade unions and the TUC was considerable. Employment legislation from 1980 together with economic recession has led to a dramatic reversal of these trends (Lewis and Simpson 1981; Clark and Wedderburn 1983). The issue of the extent to which there is consensus about health and safety between management and unions is also relevant. Opposing views are found in Robens (1972) and Nichols and Armstrong (1973) and are dealt with briefly in Dawson et al. (1984b).

What Actually Happened

The plant continued much as described. It stayed in business. The accident rate began to give serious cause for concern and information on health hazards suggested some workers faced considerable long-term risks.

Answers

1 For each of the roles (i.e. (i) and (ii)) given, consider the actor in terms of the resources they have (expertise, qualifications, experience, credibility, collective support, control of access to powerful patrons, personal status, legal and organizational rights, rules and procedures), and the constraints and limitations under which they operate. A brief summary of relevant factors is given in Table B. Different teachers may choose to highlight other patterns of resources and limitations, and establish different means – ends paths. One issue underlying this discussion for all actors is motivation. Why should they attempt to do anything?

2 Establish your rights and functions with reference to branch officials and other safety representatives (HSE 1977). Set out, in discussion with other safety representatives and your members, what sort of programme and structure you think is appropriate for information dissemination, inspections, committee activities, reporting back to members, reviewing progress on recommendations and actions. Use resources such as extent of union membership; support and information from branch, regional, and national union sources. Work within and yet try to change constraints deriving from the economic situation of the company (how short are resources really?), the apathy and fear amongst members, and the disinterest of the management.

3 A separate process safety committee appears to have the advantage of concentrating technical excellence for analysis and problem-solving, but this is based on two questionable premises: (a) management and experts will always agree on the nature and acceptability of risk and merely require an appropriate forum to facilitate this process; (b) workforce representatives will always lack technical and operational knowledge and will not have access to expert advice through their unions, etc. It has the disadvantage of losing the opportunity for workforce involvement, commitment and sources of operational information. However constituted, the process safety committee should report to the main safety committee, which should also have formal links with management decision making; with the opportunity for the committee to comment on rejections of its proposals or on the timetable and method of implementation, if they are accepted.

4 Yes. Line responsibility will only be secured through a combination of performance appraisal, accountability, clear encouragement from superiors and training. What about giving managers a health and safety revenue budget, with clear procedures laid down for handling applications for capital items? If line responsibility becomes stronger, the role of specialist as adviser also becomes more important.

5 Make a distinction between safety problems (which are relatively widely understood and cause accidents with obvious consequences) and health problems (which are often poorly understood even by experts and may cause illness and disability in the long term). Each requires different approaches to training, inspection, monitoring, information collection and dissemination, although there is no reason why they cannot be dealt with in the same committees and by the same specialists.

6 Invest in generating and maintaining a technically sound and comprehensive data base on hazards and how to control them. Make sure safety representatives are

Table B Framework for answering question 1

	Resources of relevance to health and safety	Constraints or limitations	Short-term goals for health and safety	Long-term goals for health and safety
(a) Graduate specialist safety adviser	Qualifications Expertise Outside experience	Ignorant of Texchem No obvious powerful 'patron' Existing patterns of authority	Rejuvenate existing procedures Support safety representatives Begin discussions with line managers on their present approaches to health and safety Institute review of standards and procedures asking supervisors and managers to consider urgent needs and objectives	Improve on formal standards Thorough review of health hazards Real implementation of policy Campaign for scheme of health and safety objective setting and performance appraisal
(b) Departmental production manager	Position, status Expertise	Other priorities (lack of will and resources) Lack of information	Initially to maintain status quo Can working methods be altered to promote safety and productivity? Consider what can be done about attitudes and motivation	Unlikely to develop long-term goals off own initiative but may develop a programme to control hazards if subject to pressure from higher up hierarchy and/or trade unions and/or inspectors. In which case may also turn more to safety adviser for information

aware of this information facility and are encouraged to use it to the full. Ensure that safety representatives are fully aware of rights and functions and give advice on their use and practice.

7 The success of self-regulation depends on the orientations of senior and line managers, on the strengths and activities of the trade unions and on the vigilance and strength of the Inspectorate. Sometimes, even in recession conditions, self-regulation works well and the application of the criterion of 'reasonably practicable' leads to the establishment of a safe and healthy working environment which is economically viable. Other times, particularly in smaller establishments, in poorly unionized sectors and in companies where everyone fears for their job, 'self-regulation' is the basis for maintaining unsafe and unhealthy conditions.

References and Further Reading

Bain G (ed.) (1983) Industrial Relations in Britain, Blackwell

Beaumont P B (1983) Safety at Work and the Unions, Croom Helm

Brown W (ed.) (1981) The Changing Contours of British Industrial Relations, Blackwell

Clark J Wedderburn K W (1983) Modern labour law: problems, functions and policies, in Labour Law and Industrial Relations: Building on Kahn Freund, edited by K W Wedderburn, R Lewis and J Clark, Clarendon Press

Daniel W Millward N (1983) Workplace Industrial Relations Survey, Heinemann

Dawson S Poynter P Stevens D (1983) How to secure an effective health and safety programme at work, OMEGA: The International Journal of Management Science 2: 443–446

Dawson S Poynter P Stevens D (1984a) Safety specialists in industry: roles, constraints and opportunities, Journal of Occupational Behaviour 5: 253–270

Dawson S Poynter P Stevens D (1984b) Resolving health and safety conflict, Management Today, April

Glendon A I Booth R T (1982) Worker participation in occupational health and safety in Britain, International Labour Review 121: 399–416

HSE (1977) Safety Representatives and Safety Committees, HMSO

HSE (1983) Manufacturing and Services Industries Health and Safety 1981, HMSO (subsequent reports will be published annually)

Kahn-Freund O (1977) Labour and the Law, Stevens

Kotter J P (1982) The General Managers, Free Press

Legge K (1978) Power, Innovation and Problem-Solving in Personnel Management, McGraw-Hill

Lewis R Simpson B (1981) Striking a Balance? Employment Law after the 1980 Act, Martin Robertson

Nichols T Armstrong P (1973) Safety or Profit: Industrial Accidents and the Conventional Wisdom, Falling Wall Press

Pfeffer J (1981) Power in Organizations, Pitman

Robens Lord (Chairman) (1972) Safety and Health at Work, Report of the Committee 1970–72, Cmnd 5034, HMSO

Stewart R (1982) Choices for Managers – A Guide to Managerial Work and Behaviour, McGraw-Hill

CASE 16 Redundancy: Office Engineering Company
Stephen Wood

Theoretical Background

Industrial Relations Theory

This includes questions of bargaining and why management might negotiate over redundancy; the relative power of management and workers, and the potential sources of power for workers in a redundancy situation; the role of trade unions as opponents of management initiatives; and the relationship between shop stewards and their members. (The key concept is bargaining power.)

Motivation Theory

This encompasses the meaning of work and the effects of unemployment, and why people are prepared to volunteer for redundancies, particularly when unemployment is on the increase. (The key concepts are the Protestant work ethic, needs and orientation to work.)

Other Aspects

These include the extent to which industrial relations is part of the overall corporate strategy; the problems of coordination amongst management; and the difficulty of disclosing information in an uncertain environment. (The key concepts are employment protection and consultation rights.)

What Actually Happened

The personnel manager proposed the following: voluntary redundancies, early retirement at 60, part-time women should be dismissed, and people given a closing date for volunteering. If not enough people were forthcoming, there would be a second closing date. If still not enough people came forward, then more women would be made redundant. As many as possible should leave on the same date. Managers and supervisors were to brief their work groups and details were to be posted on boards. There was little need to involve unions, and no scope for negotiation. Consultation during this period might help. The terms offered were above the statutory rate, and based on length of service. Productivity was bound to improve as people have to work harder for their money. The proposals were accepted by the board, except for early retirement – vetoed by chairman.

Senior union representatives got wind of the announcement, and demanded to see the production director prior to a briefing of the supervisors. The union got him to admit to the redundancies, but he said all would be voluntary. He then briefed the supervisors – by this time the workforce knew that 'something was up'. Production ceased and the union instructed the employees not to attend briefings by supervisors. The union was against redundancies, but it was difficult to mount a concerted attack – a work-in or sit-in was seen as impossible, since NOC was a major customer and people were calculating their redundancy allowances as soon as terms were given out.

Skilled men were keen to volunteer; many women saw the redundancies as inevitable; the most worried were the young, unskilled workers. The stoppage continued until lunch. Representatives decided to negotiate for a totally voluntary scheme and good terms. The management were reluctant to negotiate, but over the weeks they negotiated about: people being paid for staying on beyond date they wished to leave; allowing people to volunteer when they liked; compensation for violation of the implicit no-redundancy agreement on the move to Wales.

One hundred and seventy left, over six months. The supervisors found it hard to tighten up on discipline, as the management wanted. Overtime continued, as did inefficiencies and bottlenecks in production. Resentment and uncertainty were experienced on the shop floor – some felt the company wouldn't let them go, whilst others felt victimized at being openly encouraged to leave. Much of the administrative work was transferred to Wales; the office staff got bored and were allowed to leave, and this set off further demands from some skilled men to let them leave. So many skilled men left that the machine downtime became too great and the firm had to recruit. Two years after the initial choice of option 4, the South London plant was closed, and the site sold.

Answers

Whatever the students suggest is bound to be better than what the company did. There are no correct answers, but some pointers for answers are given below.

1   Option one represents a high risk strategy, although one could try to improve competitiveness by real changes in working practices, rather than simply by shedding labour. Option two makes sense operationally and financially, although the chairman and sales director are against it. Option three involves reducing manpower in the South Wales plant and would be poor for image and morale, so soon after opening. Option four is the best option, given the chairman's preferences plus the earlier commitment to the union that South London plant would not be closed. Partly success will depend on the extent to which working practices are improved.

2   In many ways, it is better for people to leave at the same time. It may be difficult to manage at the time, but this would be better for morale and enables people to look forward once others have left. One option is to have two leaving dates.

3   The voluntary method is better for morale and industrial relations. It is fairer and makes union opposition harder. It may cost more immediately, but is more likely to achieve increased productivity in the long run. There is a real problem that good, skilled people will volunteer. However, some will want to stay, especially those who feel their skills are firm-specific, and some may be persuaded to stay. It is desirable to involve the unions in this process – management will need to use the union to get information and advice, but the union is likely to turn such consultation into negotiation.

4   Terms above the statutory rate and related to length of service seem fairest, but the management will not want to make the terms too desirable. In some cases, the firm may be making payments to people who were ready to move and able to find work anyway. The unions will certainly want to negotiate on this issue.

5   The union will oppose redundancies, but it is in a weak position in this case, because NOC is a major customer, the market is in decline, the redundancies are voluntary and plenty of people seem interested. Union strategy will probably be limited to negotiating the best terms, but they have few sanctions. Conflicts exist between the principled opposition by the union and the self-interest of some of their members. Some union leaders may feel people are 'selling the jobs of the next generation' and will be concerned about the effect of unemployment on the locality. The union will probably make a comparison with South Wales and ask why there are no redundancies there? They may insist on certain manning levels but if enough volunteers are forthcoming, they are likely to cooperate with any changes in working practices.

6   Demand may pick up and productivity in South Wales is uncertain. It is also not certain that the Japanese will continue their expansion. Fears that the plant may close should not be ignored. The management might link redundancies and changes in working practices as a way of protecting the future security of plant. The union may be suspicious but the workforce may respond positively.

7   The main methods are as follows: to expand jobs of direct workers, and reduce indirect support jobs, e.g. less labourers, storemen, setters, inspectors, progress chasers; to increase flexibility and preventive maintenance; to make more use of work measurement to intensify labour content; reduced overtime; possible use of problem-solving groups. Considerable retraining may be required. Redundancies

could inhibit progress here, unless the management link them to changes in working practices and the survival of plant. The management may need to negotiate on these issues, but will argue for a degree of urgency.

8   Involve line managers and supervisors in the change process to use their expertise and convince them of the problem. The management will want to see this as a continuous process. It is also important to pay attention to the details of the redundancy exercise so that people are given precise information on their entitlement – this means that superiors are not faced with a disgruntled workforce or spend all their time on redundancy.

References and Further Reading

Fatchett D Ogden S G (1984) Public expenditure cuts and job loss: a union response, Journal of Management Studies 21: 207–227
Herron F (1975) Labour Market in Crisis, Macmillan
Kemp F Buttle B Kemp D (1980) Focus on Redundancy, Kogan Page
Thomas R (ed.) (1969) An Exercise in Redeployment: The Report of the Trade Unions Study Group, Pergamon

CASE 17   Management Development: British Rail
John Burgoyne

Theoretical Background

There is no single satisfactory theory or methodology which will answer in a straightforward manner the questions posed by this case. Nor is there even one which seems to describe the situation satisfactorily. Three possible theoretical approaches are listed below.

(a) *A training or human resources planning approach*   It is assumed that jobs can be described in detail, in terms of their activities and the skills involved, so that carefully constructed training plans can be developed to meet them, and evaluated, in the context of a detailed manpower plan. Unfortunately, management jobs seem too volatile and unstructured to allow this approach.

(b) *Theories of managerial behaviour and effectiveness*   Theories of managerial effectiveness seem inadequate to deal with the nature of organizations, and different views of the nature of organizations lead to different ways of conceiving what the managerial process might be, and what might constitute 'effectiveness'. Empirical studies of managerial behaviour tend to confirm that it is very idiosyncratic, and difficult or impossible to fit into any standard conceptual framework.

(c) A composition of theories and models which allows an interpretation of the situation to be developed from a 'career' theory (see Schein 1978); from ideas on organizational ideologies and cultures (see Handy 1976); and from a categorization of the possible functions of management education and development, seen from different perspectives.

Career theory   (1) Organizations are staffed by or made up of people in careers, and how they work depends on who is in what role, and with what skills, values, priorities, etc. (2) Careers have structural (what roles, in what order) and developmental (what skills, values, priorities) aspects. (3) Systematic management development is the attempt to superimpose deliberate steps to manage careers on the natural processes which shape both the structural and developmental aspects of all careers. (4) According to Schein (1978) all careers are in a sense a 'deal' and result from a negotiation between the employee and those who make decisions on behalf of the employer about the structural and developmental aspects of the employee's career. (5) There is a 'psychological contract' which is both part of and background to these 'deals' and negotiations. The dimensions of this are (a) organization-centred – the organization plans career moves, and trains people for planned moves; the individual accepts the organization's right and responsibility to do this; (b) individual-centred – organizations operate an internal 'free labour market'; individuals plot their own desired careers, apply for jobs that fit this, and seek help from the organization as necessary to develop themselves for current and future jobs.

Organizational cultures   (6) The predominant 'psychological contract' in these terms is likely to vary with the dominant ideology or culture in particular parts of an organization, as characterized by Handy (1976): (a) role culture – well-specified jobs, clear status, rank seniority, reporting relationships, work prescribed by rules and procedures; (b) task culture – work done or allocated on basis of expertise, temporary project teams, leadership based on expertise related to task, not seniority, observable performance highly valued; (c) power culture – a political climate, informal deals, understandings, negotiations, continuous process of setting up arrangements in a volatile environment, careers progress by survival of the fittest or most cunning; (d) people culture – work on the basis of collective and open process of attempting to match individuals' skills, interests and aspirations to work which needs to be done; work arranged cooperatively. Role cultures can be seen as favouring an organization-centred psychological contract over management development. Task, power and people cultures may favour greater degrees of individual-centredness.

Functions of management development   (7) The functions of programmes concerned with the developmental aspect of career management can be seen as (a) training – developing specific skills for specific tasks; (b) indoctrination – inculcating values and attitudes, including those implied by the cultures or ideologies described above; (c) education or professional self-development – individuals gaining a broader understanding of ideas and theories underlying their practices and the processes of which they are part; greater awareness of their own skills and values; (d) 'arena' – management development programmes, and the activities involved in setting them up, serve as an 'arena' in which different values, priorities, beliefs come together and are worked on.

Answers

For the reasons described above, there are no definitive prescriptions for what should be done about the issues described in this case, however, directions must be chosen, and here is one set of proposals, arising from the author's judgment in the light of the range of ideas given above. These are set out in a straightforward, prescriptive manner, to provide a focus for debate.

1   Continue to run the current programme, give it a fair trial, use it as a vehicle for learning more about management development in BR, capitalize on the investment and learning achieved so far.
2   Carry out significant experiments within the programme, especially cafeteria or resource-based methods, to gain some experience on which to base choices about more radical future changes.
3   Develop radical contingency plans.
4   Shift focus of evaluation to follow-up; test ideas on psychological contract implied above.

5 Action-research test of the hypothesis that 'learning from management development is more effective if it follows structural change directly affecting the people
   involved, rather than development provided as foundation for future, but in-
   definite, change'.
6 Increase understanding of and working links with the processes by which careers
   are planned and 'managed', with the intention of strengthening processes of planning, learning and development for individuals in this context.
7 Develop and maintain a 'view' of the relation between the management development programme, the priorities of corporate and personnel policy, continuing
   structural and organizational changes, and the related processes of management
   manpower and career planning.
8 Deliberately open this 'debate' in as many areas as possible, to serve the 'arena'
   function described above.

References and Further Reading

Easterby-Smith M V P (1981) The evaluation of management education and development: an
    overview, Personnel Review 10(2): 28–36
Handy C B (1976) Understanding Organizations, Penguin
Morris J F Burgoyne J G (1973) Developing Resourceful Managers, Institute of Personnel
    Management
Schein E H (1978) Career Dynamics, Addison-Wesley
Stewart R (1982) Choices for the Manager: A Guide to Managerial Work and Behaviour,
    McGraw-Hill

CASE 18   Payment Systems: Mayfly Garments
Dan Gowler and Karen Legge

Theoretical Background

A wage or salary system can be conceptualized (1) as the independent variable which
motivates or controls individual or group behaviours (dependent variables) (Lawler
1971; Lupton and Gowler 1972). From this perspective, see the content and process
theories of motivation, e.g. Maslow's and Alderfer's need hierarchies, for why and
when money is important to individuals; reinforcement, equity and expectancy theories
for whether a payment system in context is likely to elicit managerially intended or
unintended behaviours (Lawler 1971; Miner 1980). It can also be conceptualized (2) as
the dependent variable, in an organizational context (independent variable) which will
influence how it operates. Key 'contextual' variables for wage payment systems are
technology, labour markets, disputes and dispute procedures, structural characteristics
(see Lupton and Gowler 1969); for salary systems, labour market and organizational size
and structure (Lupton and Bowey 1983, Chapter 5). Payment system design involves
securing a 'match' between a payment system and its context, so that the motivational
principles embodied in the payment system are not underminded by the organizational
situation in which it has to operate (Legge 1974; White 1982, Chapter 18). Conflict over
pay can reflect issues of payment system design in addition to those concerned with pay
levels (White 1981). For further case studies of employee reactions to incentive payment systems (e.g. high performance versus restriction of output, goldbricking, cross-
booking, slack standards, proliferation of special allowances, loss of managerial control

over work allocation) in appropriate or inappropriate contexts, see Bowey et al. (1982), Brown (1973), Lupton (1963), Millward (1972) and Roy (1952).

What Actually Happened

Management's strong ideological commitment to individual incentive systems made it unwilling to contemplate any redesign of the payment system. In this they were supported, in the following year, by a downturn in product and labour markets. This (a) enabled them to slow down the rate of product diversification and sought-for output expansion, and (b) slowed down labour turnover. Labour turnover was further decreased by a temporary freeze on recruitment and greater stability of the new recruits of the previous year (Asian school-leavers and older part-timers). However, when both labour and product markets became more buoyant, the problems outlined in the case study began to reappear. Management decided to withdraw gradually from what was seen as an unduly competitive labour market and acquired two factories in development areas, where unemployment rates were higher and wage rates lower than in south-east England. Taken over by a large organization, Mayfly, in the 1980s, no longer manufactures in Riverside.

Answers

1 Present individual incentive system inappropriate because (a) production process lacks 'smoothness' necessary for individuals to acquire speed and (b) fall-back rate too low, given (a). Contextual factors, e.g. number of job and product modifications, number of product changes, number of stoppages, time required to fill a vacancy, labour turnover, absence; are undermining reinforcement principles of incentive, and generating negative expectancies of $\Sigma[(e{\rightarrow}p) \times \Sigma[(p{\rightarrow}0)(v)]]$ relationships in individuals. Present scheme does little to encourage high quality, which is likely to be increasingly important, given nature of the competition, except by negative sanctions; does not encourage flexibility (required by sectionalized flow method of production).

2 Some alternatives: (1) Retain individual incentives, but increase the fall-back rate to (a) the average earnings of pre-product diversification year, adjusted for inflation or (b) the standard earnings per hour. (2) Group incentives based on the team performance, increase fall-back rate as above, or to 85% of SEL for all machinists. (3) Simple measured daywork, i.e. fixed standard bonus for fixed level of worker performance, pay maintained if performance drops for reasons beyond worker control. (4) Stepped day work, e.g. premium pay plan: jobs classified by means of job evaluation, within each range of job classification, several fixed but stepped rates of pay depending on performance level. (5) Weekly wage based on job evaluation, with no bonus. (6) Weekly wage based on the grading of each individual machinist according to skill (i.e. number of machines and operations capable of undertaking), no bonus.

3 (a) (2) and (6) above are likely to encourage flexibility. (5) encourages machinists to be flexible about undertaking high skill jobs, but to resist transfer to low skill jobs. (4) would have the same effect as (5), unless the machinist can compensate by greater speed on a low skill job. In the case of (1) the high fall-back may decrease resistance to flexibility, but it gives no encouragement. (3) gives some flexibility, but much bargaining about the 'reasons beyond worker control'. (b) Payment systems which encourage flexibility may optimize team output levels, assuming adequate training support and supervisory maintenance of at least standard effort

levels. Payment systems in which reward is not contingent on output, (5) and (6), or where a theoretical contingency is undermined by excessively high fall-back rates, (1a), or by union bargaining over 'reasons beyond workers' control', (3) and (4), can result in low output, if the workforce is motivated solely by money. Note that (2) may result in decreased output of the most productive workers if they feel they are 'carrying' the less productive. (c) None of the payment systems above promote quality, except through negative sanctions. It is arguable that quality is best encouraged through training or socialization or supportive supervision, as in the Japanese model. (d) Depends on machinists' perceptions of adequacy of levels of pay and availability of alternative jobs, rather than the design of the pay system itself. Resist overtime, because of the overtime–absence substitution effect (Gowler 1969; Legge and Hilling 1974, 1975). (e) Where reward in theory or practice is no longer contingent on output, chargehand will have a larger role in maintaining effort levels. Role conflict where motivating workers to reach higher performance is combined with disciplining them or bargaining over failure to reach contracted performance, as in (3) and (4). (See also (c); Gowler 1970.) (f) Payment systems which secure the highest productivity are likely to produce lowest unit costs, and vice versa, irrespective of actual level of pay.

4   If management insist on individual incentives: (a) This would result in a need for more planning to allocate homogeneous work to teams; are all the product modifications necessary? (b) Either (i) recruit machinists less likely to leave if pay drops (non-unionised labour, poor English speakers, those motivated by reasons other than pay, school-leavers 'giving-in') (Legge 1970; Johnston 1981) or (ii) select experienced machinists. (Note that (i) and (ii) may be incompatible.) (c) Involve chargehands more in (a); emphasize the administrative role and discourage 'helping out'. (a) and (b) (i) should improve morale and motivation; (a), (b)(ii) and (c) should improve productivity.

   If management will accept group incentives: (a) experiment with semi-autonomous work groups (SAGs) (see references for Case 1). (b) Allow the team some role in selecting into their SAG. Emphasize training, rather than specific external recruitment policies. (c) The elimination of the chargehands' role in light of (a). Possibly introduce a facilitative role, concerned with training, coordinating work allocation to teams, liaising with other departments etc. Ex-chargehands to be trained for this role? (a) and (b) should improve morale and motivation, and may improve productivity; (c) should improve productivity, but may be resisted by chargehands, if they feel unable to cope with the new role.

5   In general, strategies aimed at reducing environmental uncertainty (see Galbraith 1973). Possibly a marketing solution, if the organization can identify a specialist niche, which might be less sensitive to cost and more sensitive to quality. However, this would also be likely to have implications for the payment system (e.g. a move to a high day rate).

References and Further Reading

Bowey A M Thorpe R Mitchell F H M Nicholls G Gosnold D Savery L Hellier P K (1982) Effects of Incentive Payment Systems UK 1977–80, DOE Research Paper 32, October

Brown W (1973) Piecework Bargaining, Heinemann

Galbraith J R (1973) Designing Complex Organizations, Addison-Wesley

Gowler D (1969) Determinants of the supply of labour to the firm, Journal of Management Studies 6: 73–95

Gowler D (1970) Socio-cultural influences on the operation of a wage payment system: an exploratory case-study, in Local Labour Markets and Wage Structures, edited by D Robinson, Gower

Johnston T (1981) Home relationships and work behaviour 11. Informal family financial relationships and productivity at work, Personnel Review 10 (4): 23–29

Lawler E (1971) Pay and Organizational Effectiveness: A Psychological View, McGraw-Hill

Legge K (1970) Paying Mum and motivation, Personnel Management 2 (1): 30–32

Legge K (1974) Remuneration: the problems of selecting and managing wage payment systems in Administration of Personnel Policies (eds) R Naylor and D Torrington, Gower, Chapter 8

Legge K Hilling S (1974, 1975) Overtime, absence and the structure of the pay packet Parts I and II, Journal of Management Studies 11: 205–223; 12: 45–65

Lupton T (1963) On the Shop Floor, Pergamon

Lupton T Bowey A M (1983) Wages and Salaries, Gower, Chapter 5

Lupton T Gowler D (1969) Selecting a Wage Payment System, Kogan Page

Lupton T Gowler D (1972) Wage payment systems. A review of current thinking, Personnel Management 4 (1): 25–28

Millward N (1972) Piecework earnings and workers' controls, Human Relations 25: 351–376

Miner J B (1980) Theories of Organizational Behavior, Dryden, Chapters 2–10

Roy D (1952) Quota restriction and goldbricking in a machine shop, American Journal of Sociology 67: 427–442

White M (1981) The Hidden Meaning of Pay Conflict, Macmillan

White M (1982) Selecting a salary system, in Handbook of Salary and Wage Systems, edited by A M Bowey, Gower, Chapter 18

CASE 19   Equal Opportunities: Champion Oils Ltd.
Sylvia Shimmin and Joyce McNally

Theoretical Background

Orthodox social scientists have generally concentrated their theoretical analyses on the behaviour of men. When confronted with a need to take cognizance of the presence of women in organizations, there has been a tendency to rely on popular stereotypes to 'explain' social, industrial and political phenomena (McNally 1979). Organizational theorists rarely address the question of sexual inequalities in organizations (Wolff 1979). A serious conceptual analysis has begun only in the last few years, largely as a result of the modern women's movement. In this context, the concept of 'patriarchy' (male dominance) is receiving critical attention (Beechey 1979).

In preparing to teach this case, a knowledge of the main provisions of the Equal Pay Act 1970 and the Sex Discrimination Act 1975 is necessary (Morris 1983). Awareness of the role of the Equal Opportunities Commission (EOC 1976) is also advisable.

The case has economic (e.g. division of labour), sociological (e.g. socialization of women and gender identities), psychological (e.g. stereotyped attitudes) and industrial relations (e.g. pay bargaining) dimensions, each or all of which may be emphasized when discussing it. Reference should also be made to the bimodal pattern in women's employment (Hakim 1979) and its consequences for equality legislation (Creighton 1979).

Another approach which may be adopted is to utilize the perceptions of the participants and, for example, consider the position of Edna, the woman shop steward and branch secretary, in relation to the position of women in the trade unions (Ellis 1981). Throughout the case, students should be encouraged to give serious attention as to how they would deal with male prejudice in situations of the kind depicted.

Answers

1   (a) The company differentiates through the allocation of jobs, in the way it uses

on-site job-training schemes; and in its restriction of overtime and shift-working to male workers.

    (b) Potentially, the company is in danger of contravening the Sex Discrimination and Equal Pay Acts in all respects (i.e. access to jobs; training, promotion, shift and overtime allowances).

2   The effects include the following: blocked access to jobs held by men, resulting in minimal promotional opportunities, and continuing low pay; nil-access to overtime and shift allowances sets further limits on earning capacity; possible psychological effects, e.g. lack of confidence and low expectations on the part of women employees.

3   Slipshod descriptions of women's jobs by departmental managers; unequal representation of women's jobs in benchmark jobs (only one woman's job); exclusion of characteristics found in women's work in choice of job factors; and grade boundary-lines drawn so as to limit women's jobs to lower half of grade-structure.

4   (a) Low job status resulting in low personal evaluation – leading to lack of confidence in ability to argue one's case and doubt as to one's actual merits; union reluctance to upset male members by promoting women's rights; fear of the hostility of male workers.

    (b) Primary and secondary socializing of girls or women into the adoption of 'feminine' personality characteristics, which militate against the development of assertiveness, self-assurance, the ability to take public action, and to challenge the traditional rights of men. Domestic responsibilities which reduce the opportunity to take up trade union work.

5   (a) An audit of company and trade union records to identify the distribution of men and women in jobs, grades, pay-levels, among lay (union) officials, and negotiating committees; an appraisal of internal and external training courses.

    (b) Principally the need for and availability of local authority child-minding facilities, holiday playschemes, etc.

6   The commitment of the organization to the equal opportunity programme based on positive action, similarly the trade union; the incorporation of the programme in collective agreements; effective communication with employees; measures to deal with anxiety in women, opposition of men; involvement of Equal Opportunities Commission to advise and/or instruct; consultation with the women about preferred hours and conditions, e.g. some women would welcome the opportunity to work different and longer hours; others would find shiftwork and overtime insurmountable obstacles to employment; the establishment of an equal opportunities committee – sensitive coopting of women; involvement of training manager, etc.

7   This will depend on what has been agreed in questions 5 and 6 but assertiveness training for women should be included. It is imperative that a new job evaluation exercise is undertaken jointly by the company and the union for which a prior condition is adequate representation of women on all the relevant assessment and review committees.

8   A monitoring committee should be established; periodic meetings with management, union and employees; regular check on male/female distributions; union to monitor numbers of women on trade union education courses and to encourage participation; regular overhaul of recommendations.

References and Further Reading

Beechey V (1979) On patriarchy, Feminist Review, No. 3
Creighton W B (1979) Working Women and the Law, Mansell

Ellis V (1981) The Role of Trade Unions in the Promotion of Equal Opportunities, EOC/SSRC

Equal Opportunities Commission (1976) Annual Report of the Equal Opportunities Commission 1976, Equal Opportunities Commission

Hakim C (1979) Occupational Segregation, Department of Employment Research Paper No. 9

McNally J (1977) Women for Hire, Macmillan

Morris J (1983) No More Peanuts: An Evaluation of Women's Work, National Council for Civil Liberties

Wolff J (1979) Women in organizations, in Critical Issues in Organizations, edited by S Clegg and D Dunkerley, Routledge and Kegan Paul, 1979

SECTION 3: Industrial Relations

CASE 20 Negotiating Behaviour: Micklethwaite Brewery plc
Linda Marsh and Richard Graham

Theoretical Background

Negotiation is a process of joint decision making undertaken in order to agree the distribution or redistribution of resources. It involves competition, conflict and communication between people and parties in both formal and informal situations. Formal collective bargaining is embedded in a complex system of rules and procedures where representatives are bargaining on behalf of constituents. Informal influences include the motives, attitudes, social skills and information-processing and decision-making capabilities of individuals. Typically, representatives prepare and plan for negotiation and are under pressure to conform to the position of their own party, broader social pressures (e.g. employment law, pay comparability) and also wish to retain goodwill towards their opponents (whilst disagreeing) for future discussions. Negotiations involve integrative, distributive and intra-organizational aspects. Additional influences are: the power of the parties involved, the cost of settlement, time pressures and stages of negotiation, and the use of third-party mediation. The case itself is located at a micro-social psychological level (e.g. skills and strategies of individuals) although the issues raised should be related to collective bargaining and industrial relations more generally (see references).

What Actually Happened

The negotiating groups failed to reach agreement. The option of going to arbitration was refused by the company on the grounds that this could result in a higher or lower award than their offer being granted, neither of which would be acceptable. They wrote to all the managers outlining their latest offer and reasons for refusing arbitration. They then went with NALHM to the conciliation service of ACAS, and agreed terms and conditions in this forum. This joint agreed proposal was put to the managers in a ballot, and not accepted. Negotiations continued for several months with little industrial action taking place. Table C gives a comparison between the updated terms and conditions which would be under discussion in today's environment (and are given in the case study), the actual claim proposed by NALHM, the company's final offer before conciliation and the terms agreed at conciliation. Note the differences in expressing the same thing between union demand and company offer.

Answers

General Review
(a)–(c) Discuss with reference to the 'theoretical background'. Key words include the following: joint decision making, resources; cooperation, conflict; informal, formal processes; individuals and groups; rules, representatives; goals, skills and knowledge of individuals; group pressures; integrative, distributive and intra-organizational bargaining; outcomes and relationships; third parties; implications for collective bargaining

Table C What actually happened

Key issue	Probable updated claim	NALHM claim	Company offer	Joint agreed offer
Basic salary	£1275 per year all grades (current lowest level £4725/year)	£90.2/week minimum wage; similar increase all grades (£2509/year)	£260/year across all grades	£260/year across all grades
Unsocial hours	£1000/annum	£1000/annum	£20/week	£3/day
Holidays	5 weeks/year	5 weeks/year	5 weeks/year	Not mentioned
Machine bonus	15% takings all machines	15% takings after rent and VAT deduction	Increase from 5 to 6.5% before rent deduction	10% takings after deduction of rent and VAT
Appearance allowance	£520/year	£520/year	Not mentioned	Not mentioned
Car mileage	22.5p/mile	20p/mile	Increase from 12p to 14.7p/mile	14.7p/mile
Pension	Appearance allowance to be included in pensionable salary	Appearance allowance to be included in pensionable salary	Not mentioned	Not mentioned
Bank holidays	Paid at double time with days off in lieu	Paid at double time with days off in lieu	Paid at double time with max. 8 days off in lieu	8 days in lieu, max. 4 days added to summer holiday
Wives' honoraria	Highest amount possible before tax at all times	Highest amount possible before tax at all times	Increase from £12.1 to £16 per week	Increase to £17.49 for next 2 months, then to £19.49
Christmas working	5% of days takings for each period worked	£5 or 5% of days takings for each period worked, whichever is greatest	Not mentioned	Not mentioned
Draymen's dispute (3 weeks lost)	Only 49 weeks to be used to calculate bonus	Only 49 weeks to be used to calculate bonus	Not mentioned	Not mentioned
New technology	£1000 per annum to allow its use			
Extended hours	Remuneration for this			

and institutionalized industrial relations (see, for example, Carlisle and Leary 1981; Morley 1981; Stephenson 1978).

Stages 1–2
After preparing for or planning the negotiation discuss the following: (a) Had the students planned for all the key issues, the other party's as well as their own? (b) Did the limits they'd set themselves allow for a WIN/WIN outcome? How wide could their limits have been? (Many people set themselves too restrictive limits.) (c) Had they guessed the others' priorities correctly and were their own reasonable? (d) Had one

party thought of creative options not considered by the others? (e) How powerful did they feel and why when they'd finished planning? (f) Did they advance any arguments which the other side could have picked holes in?

Stage 3
If the negotiation was carried out, consider these questions:

1 How did the above points influence the outcome, for example if one side raised a surprise issue or option which the other side should have considered but hadn't – what effect did this have? (a) How did each party feel about the negotiation? (Refer to student tasks.) (b) How will the negotiator's colleagues or superiors or backing group react, i.e. will they have any problems selling the deal to their colleagues? (c) Are there likely to be any problems, e.g. terms not well defined so people's interpretations could differ? What sort of implementation problems could there be with the agreement reached? (d) What are the long-term considerations of the deal? Have any precedents been set which could have long-term consequences for any of the parties involved? (e) What are the implications of not reaching agreement?
2 What sort of trouble spots arose, e.g. did one party adopt an unexpected position? If so, how did this relate to planning? Were both parties talking in the same terms, i.e. weekly versus annual rates, etc.
3 Did people use adjournments and why? If not, would they have been helpful?
4 Did people trade concessions for things they wanted? Did they give way on issues without trading? Relate to a concession strategy or lack of one.
5 Did one issue dominate the negotiation? Why and what impact did this have? Could they have used another issue as a lever to get movement?
6 Was there a lack of flexibility by one or both sides? Was this because their mandates were too limited, allowed no overlap, were unrealistic? What trade-offs were missed that could have overcome this?
7 Were fixed positions adopted too early (i.e. preventing negotiation from occurring?)
8 During the negotiation did any party pick up clues about the other side's position? Did this cause them to re-evaluate their position?

Whether or not the negotiation was carried out, consider whether the mandates allowed for agreement to be reached. If not, consider the following: (a) Did (or should) the parties want an agreement even if they had to go past their worst options on any issues? (b) What are the implications of making such an agreement for future relationships with the other party? (c) What are the implications of such an agreement for your relationships with other parties, e.g. in future negotiations within and without this company? (d) What are the implications of not reaching agreement and were these considered at the planning stage?

References and Further Reading

Carlisle J Leary M (1981) Negotiating groups, in Groups at Work, edited by R L Payne and C Cooper, John Wiley
Clegg H A (1979) The Changing System of Industrial Relations in Great Britain, Blackwell
Morley I E (1981) Negotiating and bargaining, in Social Skills and Work, edited by M Argyle, Methuen
Morley I E Hoskin D M (1984) Decision-making and negotiation, in Social Psychology and Organizational Behaviour, edited by M Gruneberg and T D Wall, John Wiley

Stephenson G M Brotherton C J (1979) Industrial Relations: A Social Psychological Approach, John Wiley

Stephenson G M (1978) Negotiation and collective bargaining, in Psychology at Work, 2nd edition, edited by P B Warr, Penguin

Walton R E McKersie R B (1965) A Behavioral Theory of Labor Negotiations, McGraw-Hill

Warr P B (1973) Psychology and Collective Bargaining, Hutchinson

CASE 21 Collective Bargaining: Car Co.
Paul Willman

Theoretical Background

The case illustrates a number of current issues. One is the problem of negotiating change in contracting organizations (Willman and Winch 1984): this involves the problems of reversing a dynamic of low trust relations (Fox 1974). Where contraction and change are to occur simultaneously there may be very little scope for integrative as opposed to distributive strategies (Walton and McKersie 1965).

A second area concerns the operation of stewards at plant level when bargaining has been centralized. Stewards tend to derive influence from control over pay (Batstone et al. 1978) and, where this is lacking, from control over the pace of work (Beynon 1973). Car Co. has tried to remove both.

This relates to the problems experienced by stewards during recession (Terry 1983). Less freedom to operate may accompany loss of influence, particularly where companies see the reassertion of control as important: but this may lead to conflict over disciplinary issues which stewards can no longer help to resolve (Willman 1984).

However, the most general issue concerns *mutuality* and the extent to which this system of joint regulation can survive episodes of technological change or economic difficulty. Company strategies may emphasize shopfloor control as a partial solution to the stresses such changes induce (Gospel and Littler 1983).

What Actually Happened

In this case, the negotiations were unsuccessful and change was eventually imposed, after ballot of the employees. The atmosphere was further soured by the dismissal of a leading union activist. As a result, the company experienced disruption of production of the M2 in the first year of production. However, this was not for want of invention by management negotiators, e.g. (i) payment for change: this was dealt with in effect, by offering to pay bonus on production of the M2 'in advance' of the launch; (ii) grading: management actually *reduced* the required level of mobility within teams, thus reducing the strength of the regrading claim.

In the maintenance area, faced by craft opposition, the company moved to 'two trades response', i.e. more rapid response to breakdown by redeployment of existing skills, rather than destruction of craft-based skills. However, the removal of 'mutuality' was opposed by all of the union side.

In the longer term mutuality disappeared, and the 'right to manage' was reasserted through enhancement of the role of the supervisor. Productivity improved substantially to a level comparable with major European, though not Japanese, competitors.

Answers

1 There is scope for manoeuvre on grading and payment for change issues. The

constraint of managerial style is more apparent than real: a settlement can look 'authoritarian' but in fact satisfy a number of union demands.

2 Stewards know that the cooperation of the workforce is essential for success. Their manoeuvrability is based around this. They can either (i) force you to put something to employees which they will refuse; (ii) use this threat to extract concessions.

3 You need to remove mutuality and secure continuity of production: the precise forms of work organization are mutable.

4 There are several possibilities here. The annual review is likely to be more popular with craft than production workers: this could be used to attempt to dissolve the current opposition to changes in work organization. A second area has been mentioned above: namely the use of the bonus scheme which will be established in the review to generate a payment for change.

The other possibilities relate once more to the division between local and national bargaining. Some of the changes (such as the removal of mutuality) are clearly company-wide. It might be an option to establish new practices through the annual review, using the more threatened plants where there are no investment plans to establish the new regime first. Alternatively, South Birmingham resistance could be isolated by a refusal to implement the annual review until agreement on the M2 has been reached.

5 The issues which arise here are extremely thorny. Promotion possibilities through teams for operations equate with dilution of craft skills for maintenance. It is likely that the only point of agreement between craft and general worker stewards will concern maintenance of the status quo. Negotiators must decide which group are more important.

6 Ballots have been successfully used to promote change in the past. The pressure on jobs in the area at the moment is severe, and individual employees will be looking for transfer to the continuing M2 lines. The risks of this line of action are that motivational problems may arise after the launch.

References and Further Reading

Batstone E Boraston I Frenkel S (1978) Shopstewards in Action, Blackwell

Beynon H (1973) Working for Ford, Penguin

Fox A (1974) Beyond Contract: Work, Power and Trust Relations, Faber

Gospel H Littler C (eds) (1983) Managerial Strategies and Industrial Relations, Heinemann

Terry M (1983) Shopstewards through expansion and recession, Industrial Relations Journal, 14 (3): 49–59

Walton R McKersie R B (1965) A Behavioral Theory of Labour Negotiations, McGraw-Hill

Willman P (1984) The reform of collective bargaining and strike activity at BL Cars, 1976–82, Industrial Relations Journal 15 (2): 6–18

Willman P Winch G (1984) Innovation and Management Control: Labour Relations at BL Cars, Cambridge University Press

CASE 22 **Industrial Disputes: Small Metals Factory**
P. K. Edwards and Hugh Scullion

Theoretical Background

This includes the following: (a) the indulgency pattern (key elements of which include managerial leniency in application of rules and commitment by workers to relaxed approach; plus consequences when traditional expectations are breached) (see Gouldner 1955); (b) custom and practice (the concept of transactional rule; the emergence of rules on the shopfloor which lack senior management endorsement) (Brown 1972); (c) the frontier of control (balance of influence as between workers, stewards, and managers over the conduct of work and its outcomes) (Goodrich 1975); (d) strike mobilization and vocabularies of motive (arguments used by stewards and workers in favour or against strike action; methods of mobilizing and de-mobilizing action) (Batstone et al. 1978). Main differences include the following: (a) focuses on features of the dispute which may not be recognized by participants, and which are seen as more fundamental than the overt issues, and it neglects the context of shopfloor bargaining and issues of mobilization; (b), (c) and (d) together fill out the picture of dispute organization and its location in a bargaining context.

The case study factory is described fully by Edwards and Scullion (1982, especially pp. 34–42, 162–164, 183–185, 202–214, 238–244), who explore patterns of workplace relations and industrial conflict in a comparative context. Within tradition of work under (b) and (c) outlined above, also develops some other key concepts and arguments: (i) the criticism of the 'tool-box theory of sanctions', i.e. the view that workers have available a ready-formed set of sanctions which can be deployed against management at will; instead, comparative analysis points to differences between the Small Metals Factory and other shopfloor organizations, especially on the ability to ban mobility at will, a sanction unthinkable where management controlled labour allocation; (ii) on management, difference between a general desire to rationalize (a change philosophy) and a specific attempt to foment a dispute (a dispute strategy); management stuck to a change philosophy but did not have a dispute strategy, although stewards thought that they did; (iii) the linking of patterns of conflict in general to patterns of control.

What Actually Happened

Effects of the Dispute
There were few direct observable effects. The stewards felt that they had won, but only in the sense that an unprovoked assault had been resisted, not that real gains had been made. Their view that managers were ill-intentioned and also incompetent, in that causing disputes was not the way to increase output, was strengthened. Managers had a sense of frustration that rational and desirable changes had been held back by an unnecessary dispute.

Subsequent Development
A limited amount of evidence suggests that managers later had more success in implementing change, especially in modifying a particularly troublesome demarcation between the two unions. This reflected a wide-ranging company-wide drive to regain control and raise the intensity of labour, in which the Small Metals Factory was swept up. In addition, further plant closures and redundancies weakened the unions, while also offering them hope of survival if they accepted change. The plant was eventually transferred to another division of the company, and its future became relatively secure, albeit with a smaller workforce. Without a detailed follow-up investigation the extent to which previous union controls and managerial indulgency have remained cannot be established, but it seems that some of the more extreme controls have been removed and the stewards' powers of veto over virtually every management decision substantially weakened.

Answers

1 The dispute could have the following consequences: (a) a stronger JUC and increased solidarity; (b) an increased gap between the foremen and senior managers; (c) resentment against the management and also the JUC, for not taking a stronger line; (d) more difficulties in the short-term – long-term effects depend on broader organizational and economic factors (see questions 4 and 7).

2 (a) (i) Deliberate attempt to attack shopfloor rights and provoke a strike. (ii) Use of inspection issue as an excuse to avoid discussion of new agreements; deliberate confusion of various issues to avoid settlement; irrational attachment to tradition.

   (b) Dispute reflected a clash of logics. Management did not aim to provoke a strike (NB the times when they could have done so, and absence of conscious planning regarding initiating issues in dispute) but stewards reasonably believed there was a plan. Management clung to a desire to impose formality, even though this heightened tension and was counterproductive in the short-term.

3 This was an attempt to follow through a general policy without the backing of divisional management, hence the management was unable to combat the stewards' plant-level weapons. There was antagonization of the stewards through management's unbending attitude. The loss of the foremen's confidence was less important.

4 Agree policy with higher management; adopt a less autocratic approach; develop channels of communication with the shopfloor.

5 (a) Importance of keeping members informed; solid support essential when sanctions called for.

   (b) Avoid all-out strikes if possible; deploy sanctions flexibly; monitor effects on shopfloor opinion (e.g. any resentment at loss of overtime), managerial strategy, and stocks of raw materials and finished goods.

   (c) Strengths of good links with shopfloor plus battery of sanctions. Weaknesses: isolation of one plant; inability to respond to orchestrated managerial actions; role limited to narrow issues at point of production, no lever on wider managerial objectives. (See Beynon and Wainwright 1979.)

6 The factory is not typical. The degree of sophistication in the use of sanctions rests on a powerful, well-established steward organization. Some forms of control (e.g. on recruitment and treating mobility as a concession to be freely withdrawn) very unusual. The close involvement of stewards in production process more common, but still restricted to specific sectors (especially engineering). (See Armstrong, Goodman and Hyman 1981; Edwards and Scullion 1982; Terry 1983a.)

7 Yes. More organized managerial offensive plus effects of recession enabled management to introduce some changes. Qualifications: do not exaggerate this (stewards retain some influence); plant may be atypical (evidence of universal managerial offensive patchy; effects of recession have varied between industries; shopfloor power may be dormant and not broken) (Terry 1983b).

References and Further Reading

Armstrong P J Goodman J F B Hyman J D (1981) Ideology and Shopfloor Industrial Relations, Croom Helm

Batstone E Boraston I Frenkel S (1978) The Social Organization of Strikes, Blackwell

Beynon H Wainwright H (1979) The Workers' Report on Vickers, Pluto

Brown W (1972) A consideration of 'custom and practice', British Journal of Industrial Relations 10: 41–61

Edwards P K Scullion H (1982) The Social Organization of Industrial Conflict, Blackwell
Goodrich C L (1975) The Frontier of Control, Pluto
Gouldner A W (1955) Wildcat Strike, Routledge & Kegan Paul
Terry M (1983a) Shop steward development and managerial strategies, in Industrial Relations in Britain, edited by G S Bain, Blackwell
Terry M (1983b) Shop stewards through expansion and recession, Industrial Relations Journal 14(3): 49–58

CASE 23   A 'Lock-out': Times Newspapers Ltd
Paul Routledge

Theoretical Background

This includes the following: (i) the decentralization of trade union power (Taylor 1978); (ii) custom and practice, in particular the emergence of ways of operating (Brown 1972); (iii) the frontier of control, in particular the balance of influence over conduct of work (Goodrich 1975); (iv) technological change and impact on the methods of work (Wilkinson 1983); (v) the issues of control and skill associated with new technology (Wood 1982).

What Actually Happened

Murdoch emerged as the strongest bidder in the £55 million lottery for Times Newspapers, but he was given only three weeks to reach agreement with all the chapels on operating procedures. He had a fair wind, in that all 4000 employees were under notice and faced dismissal if the sale collapsed. This time there were genuine fears that it could be the end. Murdoch's managers, all former printworkers, negotiated directly with the chapels on manning cuts, redundancies and a new disputes procedure; talks with the union general secretaries went on in parallel. While public interest was concentrated on the 'press freedom' issue of guarantees of editorial independence, the takeover negotiators got from the unions a reduction of 563 full-time jobs and 100 shifts. The composing room was practically halved from 370 men to 186 under a new technology deal that sustained NGA hegemony of the keyboard. Les Dixon, president of the NGA, said it was the same deal that had been offered to TNL in 1978. 'Murdoch had the common sense to accept it. They did not,' he added.

The move to computerized typesetting on *The Times* and *The Sunday Times* was completed within the one-year schedule set by the new proprietor, though not without some sacrifice of editorial standards; there were many readers' complaints about misprints. The Murdoch era did not immediately usher in peace on the shopfloor. There were disputes over money with NGA machine managers and electricians which halted the papers for two weeks each, and a second 'big push' for redundancies against yet another closure threat, as well as more limited skirmishes with white-collar staff and other groups. Furthermore TNL was not exempt from industrial action by the electricians in support of the nurses, and by the NGA over the Eddie Shah dispute in Warrington.

However, by late 1984, industrial relations at 200 Grays Inn Road were better than they had been for a decade. Having embraced 'bingo', *The Times* enjoyed a rapidly-rising circulation, and the company as a whole was poised to get back into profitability. Talks with the NGA and the NUJ were due to get under way on the next stage in utilizing the new technology. A new system geared to direct input was on order with pilot terminals already installed discreetly in a room just off the editorial floor for journalists to familiarize themselves with computer techniques. Privately, the NGA was saying at national and chapel level that TNL would be the first Fleet Street publisher to go front end, and there was considerable expectation within the NUJ that journalists would soon get their hands on the keyboard. Nobody expected plain sailing, but the veterans of the conflict of 1978–9 were convinced that the Murdoch management would not make the same mistakes as Lord Thomson.

Answers

1   A wide range of issues including: technological change, simplification of production process, assertion of management's 'right to manage' along with reduction of reliance on powerful craft union, control over the production process, job content and deskilling, competition between unions.
2   TNL *gained* a new disputes' procedure, a 'back-end' system of new technology, some job reductions, and NATSOPA acceptance of some computer tasks (e.g. payroll computer); but *lost* £39 m during lockout plus £15 m in 1980–1, and eventually, the titles.
    NGA *gained* retention of monopoly of keyboard, breathing space to fight new challenges, TNL respect for their authority; but *lost* £½ m paid out in dispute benefit, 40% of jobs in composing room, and opened door for eventual direct imputting. NUJ *gained* parity with The Sunday Times (average 35% increase), agreement on new technology; *lost* nothing.
    All Chapels *gained* TNL recognition of bargaining power.
3   Yes. Would have: been careful of dismissals (creates 'war mentality'); talked to the general secretaries separately; involved the TUC earlier; conceded direct input earlier; recognized chapel power.
4   One would set a one-year, *private*, deadline to get the NGA, NUJ and NATSOPA talking about direct input; test the new disputes procedure; if there was no progress one would dispose of the titles as quickly and profitably as possible.
5   The NGA would recognize that it had won a critical but small war and that a more comprehensive policy must be drawn up; *so* one would seek a joint policy with NUJ and SOGAT 82 which held out the prospect of direct input in terms acceptable to NGA. The aim is to make newspaper production an integrated operation in which craft barriers disappear, such that NUJ cover NGA work and vice versa. To facilitate this one would encourage closer Chapel links, put new technology policy to members in a ballot, reactivate merger talks with SOGAT 82 and seek closer relationship with NUJ.
6   The role of the law is limited. This is a primary dispute protected by the 1980 and 1982 Employment Acts, and is outside the scope of the 1984 Trade Union Act. A ballot is not required when there is a lock-out. The only role of law occurs if NGA or SOGAT 82 brought pressure by promoting secondary action – publishers could then sue for damages.
7   Yes. *Advantages*: ACAS respected by employers and unions and has conducted study of Fleet Street; it can propose compromises that would involve 'loss of face' if put by parties involved; it can seek common ground; TUC has played a role for many years in solving Fleet Street disputes. *Disadvantages*: it can increase pressure for parties involved to make concessions.
8   Unions and National Publishers Association (NPA) set up Joint Standing Committee (JSC) in mid-1970s to secure a framework for introducing new technology in *Programme for Action*. However, the rank and file of all unions (except NUJ)

rejected it in 1976. JSC now defunct. Not likely to be revived. Publishers implementing change on house by house basis and NPA has less influence than in the 1960s and 1970s. The unions prefer to deal directly with the publishers. The problems are not thought susceptible to a 'grand design'.

References and Further Reading

ACAS (1976) Report to the Royal Commission on the Press, Cmnd 6680, December, HMSO
Brown W (1972) A consideration of 'custom and practice', British Journal of Industrial Relations 10: 41–61
Goodrich C L (1975) The Frontier of Control, Pluto
Routledge P (1979) The dispute at Times Newspapers Ltd.: a view from inside, Industrial Relations Journal 10 (4), 5–9
Taylor R (1978) The Fifth Estate, Routledge & Kegan Paul (see Chapters 6 and 19)
Wilkinson B (1983) The Shopfloor Politics of New Technology, Heinemann
Wood S (ed.) (1982) The Degradation of Work?, Hutchinson

CASE 24   Strike Organization: Steel Strike
John Kelly, Jean Hartley and Nigel Nicholson

Theoretical Background

This may be considered under four headings:

(a) *Theories of bureaucratic organization* and the conditions under which hierarchy, clear lines of authority and standardized procedures become dysfunctional, generating evasion by subordinates, or over-commitment to sectional or sub-goals, at the expense of overall organizational goals (Clegg and Dunkerley 1980; Lawrence and Lorsch 1967).

(b) *Theories of trade union organization* and the efficiency–democracy dilemma: how do trade unions as organizations reconcile the requirements of efficient, effective and decisive organization with the requirement of membership involvement in, and influence and control over decision making (Hemmingway 1978; Nicholson, Ursell and Blyton 1981).

(c) *Theories of strikes* In so far as the strike is an extension of collective bargaining, it can be analysed into similar subprocesses, i.e. interparty bargaining, attitudinal structuring, intraparty bargaining, as well as processes of strike maintenance and member mobilization, manipulation of public opinion, countering employer moves – from this multiplicity of sub-goals the possibility of sub-goal conflict follows logically (Walton and McKersie 1965; Hiller 1969).

(d) *Theories of organizational involvement and control* Members of an organization may be involved because of coercion (alienated involvement), provision of instrumental rewards (calculative involvement), and ideological commitment (moral involvement). Different patterns of control and involvement may coexist within the same individuals and within the same organization, and may change over time (Etzioni 1961). Individual involvement will also vary as a function of the perceived probability of success of a course of action and perceptions of the numbers of others participating (Klandermans 1984).

(e) *Theories of groups and inter-group relations* These theories examine the relationship between group membership, group identification, commitment to one's own group ideology and hostility to outgroups (Tajfel 1978).

What Actually Happened

Picket marshals and membership varied in their reactions to mass picketing. Some marshals found mass picketing exciting and challenging and a boost to morale. Others did not like the tactic because their members did not want to be moved from their 'own' plant to unfamiliar territory, to engage in activities of dubious legality.

The RSC organized a number of mass pickets in the mid-strike period, but enthusiasm and numbers waned until the RSC was forced to accept that their value was symbolic (of striker determination and commitment) for the membership and the media, rather than tactical. Mass pickets were hardly used towards the end of the strike; more effort went towards interunion agreements, with some limited success. The strike ended after thirteen weeks, with a pay offer of 15.5%.

This *could* be judged a success, but the Rotherham strikers felt that more could have been achieved, and some recognized the vulnerable position the unions were now in to fight the future job losses. Intergroup relations between unions and management were tense and strained for some months after the strike, and a two-day strike occurred in Rotherham the day after the national strike over the arrangements for the return to work.

Answers

1   Effectiveness and commitment are affected by the internal and external environment, but some external factors may only be remotely under the local organization's control. One must examine scale, gravity, origins of difficulties; costs and benefits of action versus inaction; definitions of effectiveness (*yard* steel movement, positive public opinion, etc.); definitions of commitment (attitudes and behaviours). A mass mobilization of strikers would affect morale provided there were no countervailing consequences. Increasing control over strikers by the Strike Committee could increase effectiveness if the control was accepted as legitimate; if not, it could generate evasive behaviour or withdrawal.

2   Increase the rewards for involvement, e.g. strike pay; increase costs of non-involvement, e.g. social disapproval, bar from holding union office, etc. Use social networks to involve the inactive strikers through friendship groups.

3   Temporary organizations often deal with crisis, therefore operate in highly uncertain environments which require rapid decision making. Hence centralization of authority, but short hierarchy with little bureaucracy. Similarities: problems of coordination created by division of labour (Lawrence and Lorsch 1967) and differentiation of function; subgroup objectives and organizational sub-group conflict.

4   Requires awareness of actions designed to sabotage existence of the organization. Information flow problematic (subject to distortion). Decisions often made with inadequate information. Hostile intergroup relations should promote intragroup cohesion, but cohesion may be weakened by social interaction between strikers and opponents. Cohesion and strong group identification may not be sufficient conditions for membership involvement; personal costs and benefits must also be taken into account.

5   Need a strategy sufficiently broad to unite and involve wide range of individuals, but sufficiently precise and realistic to achieve results. Given complexity of environment and limited resources of strikers, RSC could have opted for more selective attack on key firms, instead of a general assault against a large number. Picketing (as against negotiating agreements with other trade unions) has two contradictory

effects: maximizes member involvement in strike and identification with strikers, but may produce similar effect amongst groups of workers being picketed, increasing *their* cohesion and *reducing* probability they will join the strike. Negotiating support from other trade union representatives avoids this potential group polarization, but low involvement of other workers in negotiation may generate weak commitment to the strike.

6   Any striker can participate in decision making, ensuring that a wide range of views is brought to the RSC; the eventual decisions of the committee enjoy high legitimacy.

7   Main features of the strike to be used in comparison: (a) workers are relatively inexperienced but highly organized in many unions; (b) the management is highly centralized for pay bargaining; (c) the industry is part of the public sector and therefore the State is involved; (d) the industry was strategic in the economy, and multiplant; (e) the strike demand was a wage rise, but with job loss as an underlying issue; (f) the strike was long; (g) the loss of the industry's product – steel – had no immediate impact because it was not a personal consumer good, and because business firms had access to alternative sources.

8   Same picketing strategy *could* be costly as employers affected by secondary picketing could claim damages; public opinion could be mobilized against the union; strikers may therefore be divided in their loyalty. Legal intervention *could* help mobilize other workers and produce heightened commitment to strike amongst the majority of activists. Main alternatives: selective secondary picketing of firms unlikely to take court action; negotiating and persuading other workers to support the strike.

References and Further Reading

Clegg S Dunkerley D (1980) Organization, Class and Control, Routledge & Kegan Paul
Etzioni A (1961) A Comparative Analysis of Complex Organizations, Free Press
Hemmingway J (1978) Conflict and Democracy, Clarendon Press, Chapter 1
Hiller E T (1928, republished 1969) The Strike, Arno Press
Klandermans B (1984) Mobilization and participation in trade union action, Journal of Occupational Psychology 57: 107–120
Lawrence P R Lorsch J W (1967) Organization and Environment, Harvard Business School
Nicholson N Ursell G Blyton P (1981) The Dynamics of White Collar Unionism, Academic
Tajfel H (1978) Intergroup behaviour II: group perspectives, in Introducing Social Psychology, edited by H Tajfel and C Fraser, Penguin
Walton R McKersie R (1965) A Behavioral Theory of Labor Negotiations, McGraw-Hill

CASE 25   New Technology: 'RM' Division
Barry Wilkinson

Theoretical Background

RM management's approach to technical change is clearly Taylorist – see Braverman on 'Machinery' (Braverman 1974) The aim is to cheapen labour, make tasks more specialized, reduce training requirements, and most importantly tighten management control over production output (quantity and quality).

Marchington (1979) provides a concise analysis of the relation between shopfloor control and industrial relations and/or collective bargaining, especially with regard to technology. Brown (1977) and Friedman (1977) are also useful here.

Mumford (1979) provides conventional managerial prescriptions (job redesign, participation, etc.) for a more 'effective' and more 'humane' way to implement technology, while Wilkinson (1983) argues that trade unions could usefully become concerned with the 'managerial prerogatives' of technical change and work organization.

Fox (1966) provides an account of the various theoretical approaches to industrial relations.

What Actually Happened

What happened next at RM is unknown to the author. What is important is that students (i) appreciate the importance of the issue of control from the standpoint of both manager and worker, (ii) recognize that technology alone does not determine task allocation, workgroup relations, etc., and (iii) be aware of the alternative policies and strategies available to management and trade unions.

Answers

1   (a) There has been a transfer of skills from the machine operator to the process controller. Machinery now operates automatically, with far less human intervention. The process controller is responsible for setting and adjusting the electronic controls – the skilled part of the job. Foremen have suffered similarly.

(b) Basic pay was slightly increased. Piecework earnings should in principle be the same, but in practice are probably reduced due to less opportunities to beat the system. The effort side of the bargain is in the operator's favour (relaxation allowance, lighter work), but note that the operator may suffer from boredom or dissatisfaction with simpler tasks. Also note that the pay–effort bargain is still daily negotiated.

(c) Work study engineers have to *negotiate* piecework prices with operators less often – in theory they now merely calculate them. Operators are also subordinated to the process controller's judgement. NB: taking control from workers may solve management's short-term problem of control, but may in the long run create a new one – controlling technical staff.

(d) There is no evidence that (a), (b) or (c) were 'determined' by technical change. Management policies and strategies provide the answer. However, managers might use an argument about 'efficiency' or 'effectiveness' to justify some of the changes – e.g. creation of a technical elite is the most effective means of ensuring efficient machine usage. This argument is questionable and should generate criticism if raised. This can lead into the general debate on 'technological determinism' (see, for example, Buchanan and Boddy 1983).

2   An answer of 'no' to this question would be likely to indicate a Taylorist perspective. This position is defendable (NB: management's success to date). Braverman (1974) would say the present approach is logical in capitalist society. An answer of 'yes' might be given by students in the light of conventional business school prescriptions (e.g. Mumford 1979). These might advise the following:

(a) A group bonus system, with a changed role for work study in providing production targets, feedback of information on production quantity and quality to groups, etc.

(b) Give machine operators more responsibilities – especially machine setting.

(c) Train operators to cope with electronic controls. Process controllers could become technical advisers to the shopfloor. Relatively slow rate of introduction and implementation of machinery allows for more internal training.

(d) Provide information on technical change at an early stage. The excuse of 'leakage of secrets' is suspect (after all, TASS (Technical, Administrative and Supervisory Staff), representing process controllers, must already know what is happening in the new development area).

(e) Allow operators an involvement in 'productionization'. In the past they showed they were capable of contributing. (NB: a solid Taylorist might wish to reduce the 'problem' of operator interference by recruiting 'green labour' for the forthcoming changes, and sacking the loose moulders.)

3 An answer of 'no' to this question would indicate a reluctance to challenge 'managerial prerogatives' on technical change and work organization (Wilkinson 1983). It could be argued that the AUEW does not have sufficient expertise in this area, and anyway potential redundancies will take up most of the union's time and energy. If 'yes': (a) The current bonus system goes against workers on the new machinery. Try to eliminate it, negotiating a higher base rate. (b) Training in the new skills would enhance an operator's quality of working life. It is also a good basis for negotiating higher grades and wages. Ultimately a more skilled membership means a better bargaining position – formal and informal. (c) This must be well in advance. Bargaining must begin before decisions on work organization are made. (d) The new arrangements mean a potential conflict with TASS. Come to some agreements as soon as possible so that a 'united front' can be presented to management.

4 This is an essay-type question which asks students to apply the three industrial relations approaches to the introduction of new production technology. A basic understanding of the perspectives is necessary (see, for instance, Fox 1966, but most industrial relations texts will suffice). The question is an open one, its main value being that it forces students to put industrial relations concepts to use.

Notes on the Role Play
Small groups should take up each of the four roles. If the tutor requires some involvement in order to offer direction, he or she could take on the role of conciliator throughout the exercise. Students should understand the *perspectives* and *interests* of their groups, and attempt to provide recommendations which will be acceptable to the other parties. Negotiations and discussions between different groups prior to the final meeting should be important. For instance, operators may wish to get process controllers and even work study engineers to put up a 'united front', while management might wish to isolate the operators.

References and Further Reading
Braverman H (1974) Labor and Monopoly Capital, Monthly Review Press

Brown R K (1977) Shopfloor strategies and reactions to change, in The Sociology of Industry, edited by S R Parker et al., Allen & Unwin

Buchanan D Boddy D (1983) Organizations in the Computer Age, Gower

Fox A (1966) Industrial Sociology and Industrial Relations, HMSO

Friedman A L (1977) Industry and Labour, Macmillan

Marchington M (1979) Shopfloor control and industrial relations, in The Control of Work, edited by J Purcell and R Smith, Macmillan

Mumford E (1979) The design of work: new approaches and new needs, in Case Studies in Automation, Related to the Humanisation of Work, edited by J E Rijnsdorp, Pergamon Press

Wilkinson B (1983) Technical change and work organization, Industrial Relations Journal 14(2): 18–27

CASE 26 **Participation and Communication: Kitchenco**
Mick Marchington

Theoretical Background

As in all industrial relations affairs, we need to begin with an awareness of management's frame of reference or perspective (see, for example, Farnham and Pimlott, 1983). The subject of participation can also be approached from a number of angles, but we need to identify the different characteristics, reasons for its introduction, attitudes of various parties and operation. (See, for example, Poole 1975; Guest and Knight 1979; Marchington 1980.) We also need to consider radical critiques of participation (see, for example, Ramsay 1980) and assessment of its consequences (Brannen 1983). It is interesting to note how participation may be blocked (e.g. Saunders 1977) and how change may be facilitated (Guest and Knight 1979). It is important to place the subject in its wider corporate and environmental context (Legge 1978; Marchington 1982; Thurley and Wood 1983) and also to be aware of recent developments on reporting in the Annual Statements. Finally, some consideration needs to be given to the role of the employee representative, especially under a regime of managerial sponsorship and when indirect participation is linked with collective bargaining and direct involvement of employees (Terry 1983).

What Actually Happened

Over a two-year period, three primary changes were attempted within Kitchenco, but there was no clearly defined rationale behind them. They were either rushed through or based upon a relatively superficial consideration of the processes or consequences, and this merely served to increase the frustration within the company. The events were as follows: (i) There was a shopfloor referendum to consider the policy of restricting Council representation to shop stewards alone. Whilst a majority voted for the changes, this did not achieve the 65% majority arbitrarily chosen by the personnel manager. Afterwards, there were recriminations everywhere. (ii) A joint training programme was organized, but despite the fact that all managers and employee representatives were supposed to attend, not all did. There were considerable problems with playing different roles during closed circuit television sessions. (iii) An advertising agency was brought in by the company to produce a new wallet-sized glossy booklet explaining the details of the participation system. Although it was anticipated that this would stimulate interest in the system, many employees felt they were being ridiculed by management.

Competition in the marketplace became more intense, there were regular changes to the technical system and changes were rushed through, often without prior consultation. The rationale of economic efficiency was increasingly used as a legitimization for noninvolvement, much to the displeasure of the employee representatives. Several key managers, who had joined Kitchenco at the time the participation system was introduced, also became disillusioned and left for better or equivalent positions within a few months of each other.

Answers

1 (a) Looks fine in theory but does not get to the root of the problem; (b) would have

simplified the representative structure; (c) would have created greater problems and helped management to divide and rule.

2 Depends on your objectives. Could be a mixture of (a) and (b) but probably not (c) unless you were out to undermine trade unionism.

3 (a) Effective if changes led to greater employee commitment or better council decisions. (b) Parts of the solutions 1(a) and 1(b) would have strengthened union organization. May have produced greater order and stability. 1(c) would have weakened union organization. (c) The management would have become better communicators and sellers under 1(a). Would have been forced to be more thoughtful and proactive in their planning and more participative in behaviour under 1(b). Under 1(c), could have become more forceful.

4 Depends upon what is meant by 'effective'. If seeking real participation, look towards the provision of more information in advance, agreed agenda, list of action points, joint chairing of meetings, training, creation of a more positive climate within the council.

5 (a) Encourage better presentation skills, sensitivity training, awareness of objectives of participation for different groups. (b) These should include financial and commercial knowledge, decision making techniques, presentation skills and committee procedures. (c) Ensure that there is an understanding of the system, induction programmes and refresher courses, improved notice boards, time for representatives to report back to the shop floor, keep management channels and presence open to the shop floor. (d) Some overlap with (c) above. Make links explicit if to keep value-added scheme. If not, consider other schemes which are more appropriate, e.g. PBR or profit sharing.

6 Should be written as would appear in Annual Report, so need to look at some of these. It may be organized into sections and should include references to the council, value-added scheme, reporting-back mechanisms, direct involvement, training, booklet, stewards committee.

7 Think through the objectives for change. Take time to create a climate conducive to change. Think about appropriate majority. Consider why people may oppose change – e.g. non-shop stewards may fear union takeover, hostility between departments. Relate to other industrial relations and organizational objectives. Implications of change.

8 Depends upon solution but be aware of the overlaps between rigidly defined subject areas. Remember to tie in your solution with other industrial relations and corporate goals. What kind of managers are needed and can they be trained or recruited? Does employee commitment matter or can one manage by fear? Implications of communications on employees and expectations for the future.

References and Further Reading

Brannen P (1983) Authority and Participation in Industry, Batsford, pp. 49–65, 116–128

Farnham D Pimlott J (1983) Understanding Industrial Relations, Cassell, pp. 50–70

Guest D Knight K (eds) (1979) Putting Participation into Practice, Gower, pp. 5–18, 287–305

Knight K (1979) Introducing participation, in Putting Participation into Practice, edited by D Guest and K Knight, Gower, pp. 267–286

Legge K (1978) Power, Innovation and Problem-solving in Personnel Management, McGraw-Hill, pp. 117–135

Marchington M (1980) Problems with participation at work, Personnel Review 9 (3): 31–38

Marchington M (1982) Managing Industrial Relations, McGraw-Hill, pp. 35–51, 150–173

Poole M (1975) Workers Participation in Industry, Routledge & Kegan Paul, pp. 48–84

Ramsay H (1980) Phantom participation: patterns of power and conflict, Industrial Relations Journal 11 (3): 61–72

Saunders J (1977) The non-consulting manager, Management Today, May

Terry M (1983) Shop stewards through expansion and recession, Industrial Relations Journal 14 (3): 49–58

Thurley K Wood S (eds) (1983) Industrial Relations and Management Strategy, Cambridge University Press, pp. 73–82, 197–224

CASE 27 Trade Union Democracy: Union Government and Union Democracy
Roger Undy

Theoretical Background

Open discussion with Michel's aphorism: 'He who says organization says oligarchy.' Does this apply to trade unions? Do leaders pursue goals contrary to memberships'? Compare Marxist arguments (Hyman 1975) with Conservative Party view that leaders are militant and members moderate. Consider distinction between 'government by members' (process) and 'government for members' (outcomes).

Use the TGWU's diverse occupational and industrial membership to consider areas for internal conflict and cooperation. Consider goals, goal displacement, incorporation (England 1981) and plurality of interests. Establish a need for the processes of government to resolve internal differences, and discuss the processes by references to the following models of democracy (see Undy and Martin 1984, Chapter 5, for fuller elaboration of relevant themes).

Model 1: Participation and Competition in Elections
Emphasizes election of all decision makers, high turnouts, competition and closely contested elections (Goldstein 1952; Edelstein and Warner 1975). Voting system should facilitate fairness; but note different systems' trade-offs between secrecy, turnout and malpractice (Undy and Martin 1984).

Model 2: Opposition Factions and Parties
Emphasizes relevant choice in elections, between competing government and opposition factions (Lipset, Trow and Coleman 1956). Relationship between different balloting systems and factionalism unclear (Undy and Martin 1984). Note factors promoting factionalism (e.g. decentralization of bargaining, homogeneous unions, ideological divisions) (Clegg 1976; Undy and Martin 1984). If good for democracy, may create problems for efficiency. The postal ballot may not necessarily result in opposition factions, nor produce moderate leaders, but may increase the influence of media in national elections (Undy and Martin 1983).

Model 3: Division of Power and Associated Checks on Oligarchy
Emphasizes the formal division of powers (e.g. executive, conference, general secretary) which check each other. Also the separation of bargaining processes from policy and administrative decisions. Note: the informal processes may prevent the formal checks working, e.g. life-tenured general secretaries can dominate lay executives with high turnover of members, particularly in nonfactionalized unions. The postal ballot may enhance this process by randomizing branch votes in such contexts.

Model 4: Internal Bargaining Between Leaders and Members

Emphasizes the informal mechanisms which allow members to challenge unpopular leadership decisions (e.g. by withholding subscriptions, picketing head office, breakaway unions) (Hemmingway 1978). Characteristic where minority interests in heterogeneous unions are not safeguarded by leadership.

Model 5: Decentralization of Decision Making

Emphasizes decentralization and local autonomy, level of decision making rather than elections. Bifurcated unions (e.g. the TGWU) may therefore be decentralized (democratic) in the bargaining channel and centralized (nondemocratic) in policy and/or administration channel.

Use these models throughout the answers below.

Answers

1 Yes: e.g. the power is divided between the general secretary, the executive and the conference; trade groups have a high degree of autonomy; bargaining is highly decentralized. But there is little organized opposition; the general secretary has powers of patronage and can dominate conference; note the differences between bargaining and non-bargaining channels. Also the answers will vary depending on perspective, e.g. of leader, activist, politician.

2 (a) (Define which posts and whether full or half postal ballot.) Postal ballot for general secretary likely to result in reduced turnout, increased secrecy, less malpractice, but note high cost of maintaining register and the fact that it may randomize voting. Periodical election may enhance general secretary's authority over lay executive.

Postal ballot for all full-time officials is likely to reduce general secretary's patronage; provide full-timers with independent power source and shift their responsibility downwards. (Use Model 3 to discuss changes in power relationship.)

(b) If full-time executive (cf. AUEW(E)) it is likely to be more powerful (Undy et al. 1981) (Model 3). But note that the issues of goal displacement and incorporation are also involved (England 1981).

(c) Yes and no (see Model 2). This acts as check on oligarchy, but strengthens the party political nature of decision making and may threaten unity. Factionalism may be associated with the decentralization of bargaining and periodic elections (Undy and Martin 1984, pp. 192–201).

(d) Discuss in context of negotiating processes and outcomes, and with reference to turnout, secrecy and malpractice. Note the other effects, e.g. it lengthens negotiating process, may limit debate, gives others more opportunity to influence votes and reduces flexibility. It is difficult to organize in decentralized negotiations without the cooperation of the employer. The process itself does not determine the outcome (Undy and Martin 1984, Chapter 3).

3 (a) Consider the cost (a postal ballot is expensive and time consuming; choice between government subsidy versus increased subscriptions versus cut services); growth (effect on recruitment if there is a postal ballot on the closed shop, on merger if leadership changes as result of a postal ballot); organization (if there is a postal

ballot of full-time officers, TGWU may become more factionalized and therefore political; unions with appointed officers may resist merger because of a fear of loss of tenure, resulting in slower growth restricting economies of scale). Question 'efficiency', in whose terms – leaders, activists, members? and implications for unity.

(b) Consider the changes as a means of legitimizing decisions and gaining membership commitment and compare them with the existing methods (i.e. dual membership and role of general secretary). Postal ballot elections of all executive members could prevent trade groups representatives winning seats on national executive, but note the possibility of changing the nominating process to reserve places. If the general secretary is identified with one faction would this strengthen or weaken the unifying role? If full-time officials were elected, would it be a possible challenge to the general secretary's authority as only elected full-time official?

4   (a) See previous answers and Trade Union Act 1984 for legal details. On moderates winning elections under postal ballot consider the importance of the environment, competition, and relevant choice; nominating processes; emergence of candidates; moral and solidaristic as against instrumental members. Use case studies of, for example, AUEW, NUS, CPSA, NUM to show effects of moderate or militant outcomes in elections. Contrast the Conservative Party and the unions' definitions of 'moderate' (Undy and Martin 1983).

(b) Consider the unions' contribution to a wider democracy – pluralist society, pressure groups, interest articulation and its relationship to their independence (note International Labour Organization convention and basic principle – unions determine own rules). What union 'privileges' (e.g. freedom to strike, closed shop) justify government intervention? (Undy and Martin 1984, pp. 213–9). Note that the intervention to promote internal union democracy may reduce wider democracy.

5   Look for a combination of models. Focus on process and outcome, bargaining and non-bargaining decisions. Design a democratic union to fit the model (see Coates and Topham 1980, checklist).

6   Should government intervene at all? If so, by what method? Compare the registration system in 1971 Industrial Relations Act with 1984 Act. Consider desirability or effectiveness of the set of model rules (applicable to *all* unions?) subsidies (1980 Act), piecemeal legislation of parts of union government (1984 Act). Who should trigger the legislation? The government directly? Or provide employers or members (what percentage?) with legislation enabling access to ordinary courts to change union rules? Should there be special courts – role of ACAS or Certification Officer in vetting union rules and procedures?

References and Further Reading

Clegg H A (1976) Trade Unionism under Collective Bargaining, Blackwell, Chapter 4

Coates K Topham T (1980) Trade Unions in Britain, Spokesman, Chapter 3 (see pp. 92–93 for a suggested check-list for evaluating union democracy)

Edelstein J Warner M (1975) Comparative Union Democracy, Allen & Unwin

England J (1981) Shop stewards in Transport House, Industrial Relations Journal 12 (2): 16–29

Goldstein J (1952) The Government of British Unions, Allen & Unwin

Hemmingway J (1978) Conflict and Democracy: Studies in Trade Union Government, Oxford University Press

Herding R (1972) Job Control and Union Structure, Rotterdam University Press

HMSO (1983) Democracy in Trade Unions, Cmnd 8778, HMSO

Hyman R (1975) Industrial Relations: A Marxist Introduction Macmillan, Chapter 3
Jackson M P (1982) Trade Unions, Longman, Chapters 4 and 5
Lawrence P R Lorsch J W (1967) Organization and Environment, Harvard University Press
Lipset S M Trow M Coleman J S (1956) Union Democracy, Free Press
McCarthy W E J (ed.) (1984) Trade Unions, Penguin
Undy R Ellis V McCarthy W E J Halmos A M (1981) Change in Trade Unions, Hutchinson
Undy R & Martin R (1983) Legislation and the election of union moderates, Employee Relations
    1983, 5 (5): 24–28
Undy R Martin R (1984) Ballots and Trade Union Democracy, Blackwell, particularly Chapter 5

AUTHOR INDEX

SUBJECT INDEX

SUBJECT INDEX